THE BASICS OF GARDENING

Alan Gemmell

Illustrations by
Oriol Bath

TEACH YOURSELF BOOKS
Hodder and Stoughton

First Impression 1979

ISBN 0 340 234 806

Printed and bound in Great Britain for Hodder and
Stoughton Paperbacks, a division of Hodder and
Stoughton Ltd, Mill Road, Dunton Green, Sevenoaks,
Kent, (Editorial Office, 47 Bedford Square, London
WC1B 3DP) by Hazell Watson & Viney Ltd,
Aylesbury, Bucks

Published in the U.S.A. by David McKay & Co. Inc.,
750 Third Avenue, New York, N.Y. 10017, U.S.A.

Contents

List of Illustrations

Introduction

The purpose of this book is very simple, namely to help you to understand all about gardening. This is a very different thing from *knowing* all about gardening, for the latter would mean that no matter what plant was mentioned under any conditions of soil, climate, light and so on, there would be nothing about it that you did not know and no question about it that you could not answer. Clearly this is beyond the scope of any man, and that is why I make the point of 'understanding' rather than 'knowing'.

Understanding all about gardening means knowing the basic principles which underlie plant growth and development and being able to apply them to a given situation and to come up with what is a correct, or nearly so, answer. Thus, generally, if you are grafting or budding, say, a rose you will know exactly what you have to do, although you may still need to learn the best techniques to use to reach the desired end. Understanding is no substitute for accurate practical knowledge, but on the other hand knowledge without understanding can be sterile and rather like knowing all the words in a dictionary but being unable to write a passable sentence.

This volume provides the background to gardening, the basic scientific understanding. Specific details on crops, flowers and trees can be gathered from the more specialised volumes which make up the rest of the series. It is for this reason that the other books are, above everything else, practical accounts of how to do things, whereas the present volume will provide the rather more general background. This does not mean that this book is not practical also, for it is, its primary aim being to demonstrate soil, climate and plant science, all the time using the problems of the practical gardener as the starting point.

The book begins with a chapter written to help the beginner plan his garden. It describes in the simplest terms the rules you should follow in order to design a garden which suits you, and the tools you must buy (or acquire) in order to do any gardening at all. The most important aspect of any garden is the soil in which the plants grow so the second chapter discusses soils and how to use them, and since no soil is perfect this is followed by a third chapter on the fertilisers and manures used to improve (the 'in' word is *ameliorate*) the soil.

If the basic factor in a garden is the soil, the purpose of gardening is to grow plants. But growing plants can be made easier and more enjoyable if you know how they are constructed and how they work. Chapters 4 and 5 therefore describe in general terms those features of plant structure and function which are of importance to gardeners.

Plants have problems no matter how well they are grown or how carefully the soil is prepared, and much good work can go for nought if pests or disease gain a foothold. In Chapter 6 a short account of the causes and effects of these troubles is given, and the techniques which have been developed to control these potentially problematic situations are described.

Chapter 7 moves into a new area, for today gardeners are increasingly using techniques of modern science in protected cultivation either to grow better or different crops or to grow ordinary crops out of season. These techniques primarily involve the use of plant shelters such as greenhouses, cloches, cold frames or even windbreaks. Such techniques create fresh opportunities but at the same time they can raise new and peculiar problems.

Finally we are increasingly aware of our environment and of the factors both social and physical which affect it and us. In the same way plants are very much affected by the ordinary environmental climatic forces and like us they face the difficulties (and opportunities) of the safe and effective use of chemical aids. Such problems are discussed in Chapter 8 as they apply to the garden and to gardeners.

Each chapter finishes by considering those questions most frequently asked by amateur gardeners about the subject concerned and are intended to illustrate how the material in the chapter can be used to answer everyday practical problems.

1

Garden Design and Equipment

It is becoming increasingly clear that the pattern of gardening is changing as the social conditions of the country change; for example, the increase in car ownership has given a freedom of movement to many people who previously had stayed at home and gardened. So the demand for low-work gardens has increased. Also, as people have become worried about the use of chemicals and their effect on the environment, they have increased home vegetable production. This increase has been accelerated by the spreading cult of the deep-freeze allowing fruit and vegetables to be stored and eaten out of season, so eliminating the old feature of vegetable growing when a glut would be followed by a long period with no vegetables at all.

However, it is also true that the type and amount of gardening you do is absolutely defined by the sort of garden you have. This is why garden design is so important, and even if you only have the proverbial pocket-handkerchief between you and the pavement there is still a place for its design in your thoughts. If you do nothing and just leave your patch to nature, you may well be storing up work and trouble for yourself.

What sort of garden do you want?

Whether you move into a newly-built house, or an old house, or even if you have been tending the same garden for years, design always starts with asking yourself questions. It is only when these questions have been answered that you can begin to do the manual work.

The first question is 'What sort of garden do I want and am I willing to devote the time, money and energy necessary to get it?' You may say 'I want a *no-work* garden'! This is possible if you have a very small area, for you just cover it with slabs of concrete and that's that. Of course you can improve on this by leaving a few gaps in the concrete or between the slabs and planting some low-work shrubs such as a standard rose, a lavender, a rhododendron, hummock plants or creepers on the wall. But a larger area, no matter how you treat it, can only be concreted or asphalted at considerable cost and, if you do not want to meet this cost, you will need to consider a *low-work* garden. Immediately, you are forced into a planning and design situation, maybe a very simple one, but nevertheless a real one for whatever you do may affect your life for many years. It may affect the value of your house, the health of your family, your relations with your neighbours. All sorts of things will follow, so the first necessity is some quiet thought and maybe family discussion.

Now ask yourself some more questions, such as whether you want to grow vegetables. If you do then the idea of a 'low-work' garden can be given up straight away for an area of vegetables takes about ten times as much energy as it takes to maintain a comparable area of grass. With vegetables you have to dig, plant or sow, weed, feed and harvest and you may even have to spray, so that they involve real work. This is not to say that you should not grow vegetables, for nothing tastes so good as your own fresh vegetables and the cost in terms of pounds is very low, but they do involve work and if you don't do it, then the crop will be poor and you'll lose money instead of saving it. If you do want vegetables, then you have to decide where to grow them, near the house for ease of gathering or hidden from the house so that the outlook is not spoiled. Vegetables near the street are easily stolen and to make growing them worthwhile at all you need a reasonable area which will depend on the number of mouths you want to feed and the things these mouths enjoy eating.

Assuming you do not want to devote the time necessary to grow vegetables and your primary demand is for a *low-work* garden, how do you then go about designing or altering an existing design. The sort of questions you should ask yourself are 'Do I want flowers, shrubs, trees? Will I be happy with grass alone and if so will it be a good lawn, a playground for the children, a drying green, or simply a rough grassy area which can be used by everyone?'

Here it must be stressed that a good lawn demands a lot of time and effort, but an ordinary, everyday, run-of-the-mill lawn is only demanding in the summer time when it must be cut regularly. Grass is probably the least demanding of time and effort of all plants if you are content with a lawn that is less than very good.

Guide-lines for garden design

All this is leading up to the core of garden design : 'What sort of garden do you want and are you willing to put the work it demands into it, year after year?' It will be plain that there are no simple plans that will please everyone, but here are some useful guide-lines :

1. A simple garden is more easily maintained than a complex one. Simplicity can be achieved by a few different kinds of plants in a few places. Thus a lawn is simple, but if you put a flower border around it although you may improve the visual effect you add to the cost and the wor':. If you add an area of vegetables or fruit to this you further improve the garden but again at the cost of more work.

2. Perennial plants such as trees, shrubs, or flowering perennials (which live for many years) are much less work than annuals (which only live for one year) and well positioned can add to the charm of the garden.

3. Straight lines are less demanding of labour than curved lines, and in a small garden of limited area are much more desirable.

4. By using climbers on trellis or wire you can add a new dimension to the garden and this is especially true in walled or confined spaces.

5. If your garden is large enough, try to design it so that it

7

cannot all be seen at once. This enables you to have virtually a number of smaller gardens each with its own character. The divisions can be made of shrubs, trees, trellis, or even simply be the contours of the ground, but they should separate different areas.

6. A garden with varying levels is difficult to maintain but can be made more interesting than a garden on one level if you are willing to do the work.

7. Trees are best kept away from the house because they grow larger and faster than you expect, and when they have to come down, it can be very difficult in a limited space. Remember also that if trees are planted as specimens, i.e. alone, they should have enough room to develop properly and show their shape.

8. Most new gardens are over-planted and as plants mature and expand many may have to be weeded out and given or thrown away. It is usually wise to plant thinly in the beginning although this may give you a weeding problem for a year or two. It also means that you can add fresh features as you go along which helps to spread the cost.

9. Buy the best plants you can afford from good reputable dealers.

10. As you design your own garden take a good and close look at the best gardens in your area and use them as indicators of what can be done. Don't copy them slavishly or your own garden will not have the character you want.

11. Remember always it is not only your garden. It is your wife's/husband's garden and your family's garden, so you should be willing to adapt your own ideas to accommodate theirs.

12. No matter how small or large your area, you should start by drawing it on paper and then mark out the paths. Remember they have to be wide enough to allow at least a wheelbarrow and maybe a lawn mower to be moved about. If you are starting married life remember prams may need to be moved. Then complete the plan by marking areas for lawn, flowers, shrubs, vegetables etc.

It may be thought that too much has been made of the amount of labour necessary to maintain the finished garden, but there is one very basic thought you should always bear in mind. A labour-saving, or low-labour, garden can be well-maintained easily and will always look better than a complicated many-sided garden which is impossible to keep at a reasonable standard simply because there is not enough time or labour available.

Finally, although it is obvious that the longer you live the older you will become, remember it means that if you move into your first house on marriage at 22 you should design a garden different from the one you design when you move into a smaller house when you retire at 60 or 65. In all cases you must be master and not the garden, so don't overburden yourself with work no matter how strong or well you may feel.

Having roughly designed the garden the next stage is to start to create it in reality. To do this a number of tools will be necessary and the rest of this chapter will help you to choose which ones you will need.

Garden tools and equipment

All garden equipment can be divided into two main categories (1) that which is essential (2) that which may be desirable or even useful but is not absolutely essential. It is the 'essential' category which will be considered at length, the 'desirable' will be described in a briefer and more cursory form.

What are classed as garden essentials will undoubtedly vary according to taste, but there are certain areas of agreement and these can be dealt with first.

1. *A garden line*. This is a very simple home-made device which simply consists of two pointed pieces of wood connected by a long piece of twine or string. One piece of wood can be pushed into the ground and the string used as a guide to mark the edges of paths, or to indicate drills of vegetables, or by using twigs or even clothes pegs to map out curved edges. If knots are tied in the string at 30 cm (1 ft) intervals it will act not only as a device for giving straight lines but also as an easy measuring rod. The twine can simply be wound around one of the wooden

ends when not in use. Make sure the wood is relatively stout and it will last for years. Cost—a few pence.

2. *A spade*. Spades have many uses, from planting trees to digging in preparation for growing many crops, to acting as a temporary edging iron for the lawn. There are three important areas of a spade : the blade, the socket, and the handle. If a good spade is picked up, held dangling loosely by the handle and the blade struck sharply with a coin, it will give a ringing sound. If the metal is flawed or badly jointed it will only produce a dull sound.

There is little doubt that stainless steel makes the best blade, is most easily cleaned and therefore is the lightest to use, so if you can afford a few good tools make sure one of them is a stainless steel spade. You should always test the spade for feel in the shop and it is wise always to remember that if it feels heavy there, it will feel much heavier when you try to use it in wet soil or clay, so if you have any doubts choose a lighter spade every time.

The socket of the spade is where the metal blade joins the

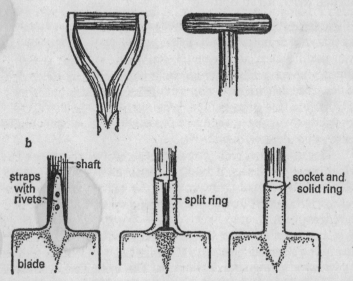

Figure 1   Types of spade : (*a*) handles and (*b*) blade fixings.

shaft and by far the strongest join is in the socket where the shaft goes into the metal. Despite this a reasonable join can be made by having metal straps running up from the blade between which the shaft is fixed with one or more rivets. The most suspect join on a spade is where the shaft simply fits into the steel plate which has been pressed around it to form a split ring (see Figure 1).

Sometimes the metal blade ends in a spike or tang which fits into the centre of the shaft and the base of the shaft is then stiffened with a ferrule of steel. This and the split ring are adequate for light work, for example with a trowel, but a digging spade needs a very solid join.

The handle can be shaped like a T or triangular. This is entirely a matter of taste but the T has fewer joins and so may be stronger. Finally, spade shafts and handles may be wood or plastic and here again it is a question of taste and feel, but make certain there are no rough edges in the gripping area or they will cause sores and blisters.

3. *A garden fork*. This, in lighter soils, is often used in preference to the spade, but be sure it has four prongs which are round or square in section if it is for general use. Forks with flat prongs (or tines) are only useful for potato digging.

4. *A wheelbarrow*. There are many versions of the wheelbarrow but the metal ones with a single wide wheel are eminently satisfactory. Once again don't be tempted by sheer size, for a full wheelbarrow is not only difficult to push but it may leave ruts in the ground. The grips should fit the hand comfortably and the feet should be solid so that the whole is stable and does not easily topple sideways.

5. *The rake*. The shaft of the rake should be about 155 cm (5 ft) and the metal head should have ten square or round-section teeth. Although the rake is not used for heavy work, the tang and ferrule method is the best jointing system for head and shaft (see above).

Many garden accidents involve rakes and these are usually the result of carelessness with the rake being left lying on the ground with the teeth pointing up. The teeth should always point down and when not in use the rake should be hung on two nails and not left head down on the floor of the shed or garage.

6. *Pocket knife.* A good sharp knife is very useful, preferably with a handle which can be gripped quite firmly. If it has a locking ring to stop the blade snapping shut it will be much safer and you should buy a stout simple model rather than a complex multi-bladed type.

7. *The hoe.* The most serviceable hoe has a blade which you use parallel to the ground and just below the soil surface (the Dutch hoe). It is a very good weeding instrument as it severs or up-roots weed seedlings and, if hoeing is done in the morning, the heat of the day will ensure their death. Stainless steel is essential here and if it is double-edged you have a nearly ideal tool (see Figure 2).

8. *Watering can.* The simplest and lightest are made of plastic, usually hold 9 litres (2 gallons) and will give years of service. The only general advice is to make sure you wash them out carefully and thoroughly especially if you have been spraying your roses or killing weeds with chemicals, otherwise the next time you use the watering can you might do a great deal of harm. A garden bucket is also useful.

Of course there are many other tools of more specialised use, such as lawn-mowers, secateurs and saws, but those listed above are the essentials. There are also one or two guide-lines for tool maintenance and purchase. Most general guides for shoppers make the point that you only get what you pay for, and for this reason it is usually false economy to buy cheap or second-hand tools. If you can afford them always buy tools made of stainless steel for not only will they last longer but they will actually make the job easier. The reason for this is that soil does not stick to stainless steel and so tools such as spades and hoes move through the soil more easily. Further a good steel tool will keep its edge longer so that secateurs, spades and pruning saws all need less effort to use than if they were rusty and therefore blunt.

Every tool should be cleaned and oiled at the end of each session in the garden. All you need to do after cleaning is to

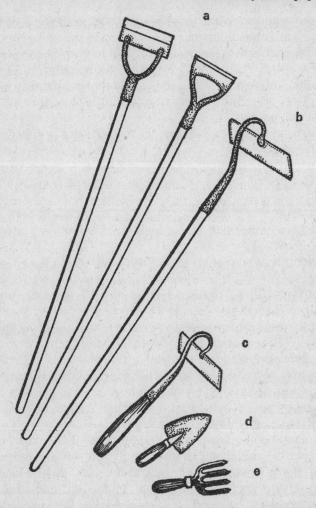

Figure 2 (*a*) Dutch hoe, (*b*) draw hoe, (*c*) onion hoe, (*d*) trowel, (*e*) hand fork.

give the metal parts a wipe over with an oily rag that you can have hanging in the tool shed. If this is done then you will find the start of your next gardening session will not be delayed while you try to scrape off dry caked mud.

If the equipment has moving parts, for example, a lawn-mower, then annual servicing is essential and should be done in the off-season, that is the winter for lawn mowers and the summer for rotary cultivators. Regular servicing, oiling and even sharpening of all tools will save hours in the end and may even save plants since little damages a rose bush more than rough jagged pruning cuts.

Finally, as far as possible store the tools in a dry shed in order to reduce rust.

Common problems and queries

1. *I have moved into an old house with an existing garden; what should I do?*

The first thing you should certainly do is wait for at least a year before making any alterations at all. A complete season will have to pass before you can even see what is growing in the garden so that rushing into digging or altering it may destroy valuable plants which were not in season when you occupied the house. The second thing you should do is think why the previous owner designed the garden the way he did. Certain shrubs may be to hide an ugly vista or to screen the garden from prying neighbours and it is only when you can get into the previous owner's mind that you will find whether the reasons he had for certain things apply to you also.

Another useful piece of advice is to proceed slowly and work to a plan, so that at all times your garden will be pleasure-giving. If you try to do everything at once (*a*) you will have a large outlay of money and labour all in one year and (*b*) until all the new ideas have settled down and taken shape your garden may be an eyesore or even a worry.

It is also as well to remember that your ideas about one part of the garden may be affected by the behaviour of another part, so that although you have a scheme on paper which is what you want, be prepared for amendment and change. Every living thing evolves and changes as it grows and you should let your garden do the same.

2. *How should I deal with a new garden round a new house?*
As described in the body of this chapter, make a map of the garden area, decide the kind of garden you want, and lay out the paths. Many new home owners then dig the paths out and put all the old stones, bricks etc., left by the builders into the trenches so produced. This ensures that the paths will drain when you eventually put the surface on them.

If the ground is very wet, try to drain it to the best of your ability with simple tile drains. It is fairly easy to put drains in empty soil, but very difficult to drain a semi-established lawn or to put drains among the fruit bushes you are trying to establish.

You then proceed by planting very few valuable or permanent subjects in the first year or so. Rather sow cheap annuals, such as lobelia, alyssum or tagetes (French marigold), grow coarse vegetables such as potatoes, sprouts and cabbages, get the ground ready for the lawn area, and generally reduce the weed population by regular hoeing and digging out if necessary.

A slow approach of this kind will also give you the feel of your garden and will provide an insight into the range of soil types which is often surprisingly large even in a very small garden. This information may help you in finally deciding the plan for your garden and may even lead you to make some changes to it.

3. *I know about the essential tools, but what about those which are not essential but very useful?*
As well as the Dutch hoe which has already been described, and which is useful for weeding, there is the draw hoe which can also be used for weeding but is more often used for drawing drills. The draw hoe has a blade which is often at right angles to the plane of the handle and so you can work backwards drawing the hoe along the surface of the ground, leaving a shallow trench or drill. The width and depth of the drill can be varied by altering the angle at which you hold the hoe and the downward pressure you exert on it.

The draw hoe can also be used for killing tough perennial weeds but if put to this purpose it is used as a kind of chopper. There is a small draw hoe with a short blade and handle called

15

an onion hoe as it used to be used for weeding between onions, and this is useful also for any weeding in a confined space.

There are many varieties of shape of blade, some one-edged, some two-edged, and all have advantages and disadvantages, so when you buy a hoe don't take the first one you are offered but examine the range, and then choose the type you prefer in stainless steel.

There are many little fiddling jobs in the garden and for many of these a trowel is very useful. This tool can be used for planting bulbs or rooted cuttings, for filling flower pots, for splitting clumps of perennials such as polyanthus. For splitting clumps a hand fork can also be very useful as the spaces between the tines allow small plants to be lifted without severing nearly all the roots. A hand fork can also be used for loosening compacted soil where there is little space as in a flower bed or in a rockery.

Both trowel and hand fork should be measured so that they can be used as quick guides when transplanting. Each is usually about 22.5 cm (9 in) long, and this principle is used widely by blind gardeners (and there are very many) who know the length of all their tools and can use them as ready-made measuring devices.

4. *If I have to buy a lawn-mower, what type should I get?* Tools in which you provide the power usually mean hard work, therefore hand-driven mowers are for two types of gardener (1) those who are young and energetic and actually enjoy pushing the mower and (2) those whose lawn is of the small pocket-handkerchief-type and for whom a power-driven mower would really be a waste of money. For all the others some form of engine to do all or some of the work is a necessity. Mowers can be driven by electricity or by a petrol-driven engine.

Electric mowers may be powered by either a direct lead from the domestic electricity supply or by batteries. When driven from the domestic supply the limits of the area which can be mown are set by the length of electric cable available. Of course, one can get many yards of cable, but the longer the lead the greater becomes the danger of it being damaged or cut as it trails along the ground. Most people therefore restrict such mowers to small areas of grass close to the house from which the supply usually comes.

The alternative to the long cable is for the mower to be powered by batteries. Such batteries are very heavy and a lot of the power they produce is used in transporting the batteries themselves over the lawn as it is mown. The duration of cut which comes from a fully charged battery is therefore limited, but small lawns at a distance from the house may be conveniently cut in this way. The snag with batteries is that they have to be re-charged after each cutting session. In a well-organised home, with a trickle-charger in the garage or kitchen, this is easily done, but it may lead to some inconvenience if the heavy batteries have to be carried around. Another snag about heavy battery mowers is that they tend to sink in the ground and leave ruts or ribs if the soil is at all wet.

The great advantage of electric mowers is that they start very easily—simply by flicking a switch. Also they are very clean with no attendant danger from the storage of smelly petrol, in or around the house. These can be very valuable points, especially if there are small children about, so electric machines should not be dismissed out of hand.

Easily the most popular powered machines are driven by petrol engines. These are very efficient and in their many forms, from ordinary to rotary to floating, do a very good job indeed. The main problem which arises is that of starting the engine. At certain times of the year, especially spring and autumn, the machine may only be used every two weeks and it is asking a lot of a machine (usually with one cylinder) to fire and so get going immediately each time it is needed. The moral is clear; the petrol driven mower must be well-maintained and serviced if the owner hopes to get good service from it! This means that it must be cleaned and checked after each cutting and the grass clippings which tend to collect in every corner carefully brushed out. Of course, the better the make then the more reliable the machine, and reliability is the *sine qua non* of a mowing machine. I know of nothing more frustrating than after waiting for days for the right weather to cut the grass to find that the machine won't start.

It is possible to buy expensive mowers with self-starters, but these are based on a battery to provide the initial spark and so the weight problem arises. Such machines are usually large with sit-on facilities.

To sum up, the kind of mower you buy will again depend on the kind, size and location of your lawn. All mowers are good in some respects and bad in others, so 'you pays your money and you takes your choice', wisely, I hope.

See also the companion volume on lawns in this series.

2

The Soil

Introduction

To every gardener the soil is the basic material with which he
works and whether it is good or bad, fertile or infertile, hot and
dry or cold and wet, it affects everything he grows and in many
cases how he grows it. It is very necessary then to get the soil
just right, or as near as is humanly possible, in order to get the
best crops in the easiest way.

It must be said at the outset that soil will repay any work
put into it, for it cannot just be left alone to do its best. It has to
be treated properly and the purpose of this chapter is to inform
you about the basic nature of the soil and how the good and
careful gardener can improve everything he grows by improving the soil he grows it in.

The materials of the soil

(a) Rock particles
It is a matter of common observation that soil is made up of a
very large number of small, in some cases very small, particles.
These are fragments of the original rock from which the soil is
derived and they affect many of the soil's characteristics. The
most obvious of these is soil drainage and the simplest approach
to this is to imagine a bucket filled with footballs and another
filled with golf balls. Of course there will be fewer footballs
than golf balls but that is not really the important thing, for if
you examine the spaces *between* the footballs and the spaces

between the golf balls then you see that simply because footballs are big they cannot be packed very closely together. In consequence there are large spaces between the footballs, whereas the spaces between the golf balls are very much smaller.

Now use your imagination to think of the particles of rock as tiny balls. Clearly the space between big particles is greater than that between little particles and *water drains through spaces*. Thus whether a soil drains well or not can depend to a very great extent on the size of the rock particles from which it was formed.

We will return to the question of drainage and particle size later, but first we must consider another aspect of these rock particles, namely their chemical composition. There are many different kinds of soil, with very many different chemical characteristics but for the ordinary gardener these fall into two categories: those based on chalk and limestone and those based on other rocks.

The importance of this division lies in the fact that the first category, chalks and limestones, contains the element calcium and the presence of quantities of calcium (or as the gardener would have it, lime) in the soil means that a number of plants cannot be grown well. Such plants as azaleas, rhododendrons, many heathers, camellias and others of the same family, are intolerant of calcium and are called *calcifuges*. There seem to be a number of reasons for this intolerance but in most cases it is based on a shortage of iron in these soils.

Such iron deficiency leads to visible symptoms and affected plants will have yellow sickly leaves instead of deep rich green leaves, and will bear poor fruit. Plants of this type are said to be *chlorotic* or suffering from iron deficiency. This condition is easily cured and a regular application of chelated iron compounds (such as sequestrenes which can be bought in most garden centres) will speedily do the trick. However, sequestrenes are expensive so it is wiser if you are in a limestone area to avoid calcium-intolerant plants such as heathers and azaleas, and to grow plants such as viburnum and clematis which revel in this type of soil.

(b) Soil water and soil air

For plants to grow at all they must have water, for this is the liquid in which food moves into the plant in much the same way as blood moves our food materials round our body. Plants can get some moisture from the air, but the bulk of it must come from the soil. But soil will never yield all its water to the plants, so that as a soil dries out, it will cause the plant to droop and wilt long before the soil is bone dry.

Where do we find the water in the soil? In a very wet soil all the pore spaces are filled with water and the roots of the plants find an abundant supply, but, as the soil dries out, the water in the pores goes and all that is left is a thin film of water surrounding the solid rock particles. This water is not easily available to the plant as it clings to the surfaces very strongly. Fortunately there is another source of soil water supply for roots, namely the soil humus, but we will come to that in a moment.

Another very important thing about soil water is that it plays a kind of hide-and-seek game with soil air. It is easy to see how this is if you imagine a pore in the soil filled with water. If you then imagine the water being slowly drawn off by plant roots, the space left by the water will be filled with air from the atmosphere. Thus a flooded soil has no soil air and a completely dry soil has lots of air but no soil water. Soil air is very important to plant roots for they use the oxygen which it contains much as we use oxygen, namely to burn up food and supply them with energy. This energy the plant uses to extract mineral salts and other things from the soil. The ideal soil therefore will have both a good water supply and ample quantities of soil air. This balance is achieved by the presence of humus which has many remarkable properties.

(c) Soil organic matter and humus

In any fertile soil there is a lot of organic matter which can be either living or dead. Both are equally important, for the dead organic matter acts as food for the living organic matter and then, as this in its time dies, it is used as food also. The life in the soil exists in very many different forms from large rabbits and mice through insects and fungi down to earthworms and to bacteria. All are important, for together they form a balanced community, but in the end pride of place must go to the bacteria for it is by bacterial action that the remains of all the larger organisms are changed into humus, the organic material which, along with particles of rock, is necessary for a fertile soil. The dead organic matter in soils is made up of fallen leaves, roots, insects, worms, and the corpses of higher animals. In fact the dead organic material is simply these corpses plus (and it is a very important plus) the compost, straw and any other material which the gardener brings into the garden. The compost he puts in the soil is eaten and broken down by insects, earthworms and fungi and then these are turned into humus by bacterial action. But humus does not stay in the soil forever, for other bacteria break down the humus turning it into carbon dioxide and water (both of which are lost to the plant), but at the same time releasing chemical substances such as potash and phosphate for use by the plants.

Humus has two other functions in the soil. Firstly it acts as a kind of cement which helps to stick the rock particles together. This means that it leads to the formation of bigger particles or 'crumbs' which will have bigger spaces between them thus allowing more water and air into the soil and at the same time improving soil drainage. A humus-rich soil is therefore a well-drained soil.

But humus is not just a kind of soil cement, for it is spongy and fibrous in texture and so holds soil water as a sponge holds bath water even if the bath is empty. The water however is not held very strongly and plant roots can easily tap this source of supply. In a good soil therefore there are large pore spaces filled with soil air, but there is a whole reservoir of water held conveniently in the humus on which the plant can draw at any time.

The interaction of the soil types

(a) Clay soil

In a physical sense the rock particles in soil can be quite visible to the naked eye as in a coarse sand or gravel, or can be very small indeed. If the particles are very small we have a clay soil with all its problems, for the spaces between the very tiny particles are very tiny also and water is held very strongly indeed in these small pores. Thus clay soils are wet and so are heavy and difficult to work. Because they hold such a lot of water they heat up very slowly in spring and crops grown on them tend to be late.

As clay soils dry out the particles tend to stick together, so that a dry clay soil is like cement and very hard to work. It is also evident that clays expand when wet and shrink when dry, and if there are plant roots in a soil which is expanding and contracting, these roots may get broken and the plants suffer serious damage.

Clay soils however have one great advantage, for they are very rich in minerals which are dissolved in the soil water and can be used by plant roots. It is important therefore to use this good point to best advantage and this is simply done by incorporating as much humus in the soil as possible. The humus will bind the clay particles together making them larger so that drainage will be improved. A heavy clay soil which is heavily composted and well worked to incorporate the humus evenly can become very fertile indeed.

(b) Sandy soil
At the opposite end of the scale is the coarse sandy soil through which water drains very quickly, carrying away all the plant food, and which in the summer may become dust-dry. Sandy soils are easy to work (for you are not digging great soaking wet clods of earth) and because they tend to be dry they warm up very early in spring.

Their disadvantages are their susceptibility to drought and their ravenous appetite for fertilisers. But here again humus can work wonders. Because humus will act like a sponge it will hold a lot of water even in the sandiest soil and in this water the fertilisers you add will be held for some time. It is a strange fact but true that the best treatment for both clay and sandy soils is the application of as much humus as you can lay your hands on.

(c) Other soils

With very few exceptions all other soils are blends of clay and sand and the account which has been given is applicable in varying degree.

The only important exception is the peaty or mossland soil. These are not very common outside the Fens and a few areas in the wetter parts of Britain such as the Highlands, the Lake District, and much of Ireland. Here the problem is simply one of wetness (because humus holds water and these soils are practically all humus) and of low fertility; since there are virtually no rock particles in this soil there are therefore none of the mineral salts the rock contains.

The solution to peaty soils is simple in theory but expensive in practice. Firstly improve drainage even at considerable cost. This may mean you have to dig tile drains or even trenches which you fill with stones in a herring-bone pattern. Make sure that the side (lateral) drains lead downhill to a main drain and that the main drains lead to an outfall such as a ditch. If no ditch is available then the drainage system should lead to a deep pit half-filled with rubble and then covered with soil which will act as a sump.

Secondly, add lime in the form of hydrated lime or crushed limestone at about 280 g/m² (8 oz/yd²) in order to reduce soil acidity. This should be done each winter preferably during digging.

Thirdly crops will grow well if you give them plenty of artificial fertilisers such as Growmore. Organic fertilisers can be used if you prefer them but the peaty soils are so organic in themselves that this particular type of fertiliser can be an expensive luxury.

pH and the soil

There is a great tendency among amateur gardeners to talk glibly about pH and its significance. While pH is undoubtedly important it must be stressed that most plants are remarkably tolerant of pH and will grow over a wide range of soil pH. The exceptions to this are the lime-haters but these have already been mentioned. What is this magic symbol pH? It is simply a numerical measure of the acidity or alkalinity of a soil, the scale being based on the number of hydrogen (or more acurately on its counterpart hydroxyl (QOH) ions in the soil. The convention makes pH 6.8 neutral i.e. neither acid nor alkaline. Numbers below 6.8 are increasingly acid and numbers greater are alkaline. Thus pH 4 is very acid and pH 9 very alkaline.

Most British plants including vegetables grow best in a slightly acid soil of about 6.5 pH, and there is a tendency for all our soils, even the chalk, to drift in an acid direction. This is because rain tends to wash alkaline substances downwards in the soil and if you measure the pH of the very surface soil of chalk grassland you will find it quite acid. With continued cultivation therefore our gardens get a lower and lower pH and it may be that after some years they may become too acid for good growth. Applications of hydrated lime will reverse the trend.

It is simple to buy a pH testing kit which, by means of an easy colour test, will tell you the approximate pH of your soil and the quantities of hydrated lime necessary to correct it. But do not be misled into thinking that a good pH will ensure good results for this is only the beginning and good cultivation is absolutely essential.

Common problems and queries

1. Is soil essential for plant growth?
Strictly speaking soil is not essential for plant growth and so long as there is a medium which contains air, water and plant food then the crop will grow perfectly well. This is the logic behind the science of hydroponics which simply involves growing plants in aerated nutritive solutions. This can be very successful. A similar logic leads to the use of no-soil composts and gro-bags. The difficulties in the wider usage of these techniques lie primarily in cost, because usually the soil is free whereas all other techniques demand a capital outlay. A second difficulty arises from the fact that soil is highly stable and it is not easy to ruin it, whereas a hydroponic solution only needs one chemical to be wrongly calculated or the aerator to break

down and the crop can be lost. It is often difficult to support plants upright in artificial situations because there is not a deep enough layer of the medium to sustain a deep root anchorage or the medium itself may be too light and puffy. Nevertheless, in special situations such as rocky islands, or on patios, balconies and roof gardens, plants can be grown very well in purely artificial soils. So the answer is 'We do not need soil to grow plants, but it is cheaper, more convenient, and much more foolproof than any other medium.'

2. *Should I dig the garden or not?*

I wish there were a simple answer to this question. It has always been the tradition to dig in the garden and plough in the fields for a number of reasons. It was said that by digging and leaving the ground rough, the frost and rain would aerate the soil and help to improve the crumb structure. Further, by digging you could bury the weeds and compost or bulky organic manure and it would break down more quickly. It was also claimed that regular digging and inversion would loosen the soil and make it more uniform and easier for roots to penetrate.

Recently all these so-called benefits have been called into question and it is a matter of ordinary observation that wild plants grow perfectly well under natural conditions without any digging at all so that the benefits of digging cannot be as great as were once thought.

On the positive side there is an aesthetic appeal about a nicely dug plot, but heavy rain pattering on unprotected soil has been shown to destroy and not improve soil structure. Undoubtedly digging can be used to incorporate organic matter in the soil, but if this is spread thickly on the surface the earthworms will pull it under and the bacteria break it down. So the question is wide open and the most sensible answer seems to lie in the moderate line. If your soil is heavy and wet then it may pay to break it up and bury compost by digging but if your soil is light and sandy then whether you dig or not almost becomes a matter of the appearance of the garden in winter. If you like it neat and tidy then dig. If you are happy with winter weeds and so on, then leave it alone and simply fork it lightly in the spring or spread a thick layer of compost on the surface and plant and sow in that.

3. *What is the value of mulching?*
A mulch is simply a thick layer, usually of peat or compost, which may be spread on the soil surface around the base of shrubs and trees. This undoubtedly has considerable value for it can act as a weed smother and prevent many weed seedlings reaching the surface before they die. Weeds which do grow in the mulch are easily removed as the roots are not so tightly buried in the soil.

If the mulch is applied when the soil is moist or wet, then it will help to conserve moisture not only because it will absorb moisture and prevent it draining away, but also because by covering the surface it stops the drying action of the sun and wind. To prove this just lift a stone—almost certainly the soil beneath it will be damp. A particular benefit is gained from mulching in the case of surface-rooting shrubs such as azaleas, rhododendrons and clematis, for the mulch, by keeping the surface layers cool and moist, provides what gardeners call a *cool root run*.

Mulches are particularly beneficial if they are applied in late spring or early summer when the soil is wet. Any fertiliser should go on before the mulch so that it can penetrate to the roots, and the thicker the mulch the better. Thin sandy soils or borders against walls or any area where drainage is likely to be fast, as at the foot of climbing roses or clematis, are good spots for mulching.

Many substances can be used for a mulch but the three most common mulches are composed of compost, peat, and shredded bark. Of these only the compost contains plant food, the other two act in the long run to improve the soil when they are broken down by the bacteria and become humus.

4. *Does the soil affect the quality of produce?*
The answer here must undoubtedly be 'yes' but not in the easy glib way that the question is often answered. 'Quality' is very difficult to define. Many people remember the potatoes or roses of their youth with a particular nostalgia which lends enchant-

ment. Because of this they tend to think that the 'quality' of nearly everything has gone down and of course they then blame modern techniques of gardening and in particular the soil treatments. It is simple to show that modern cropping methods give higher yields, and arguments used by traditionalists must therefore be based on quality.

Once again the answer lies in the obvious point that a poor soil will grow less productive crops. For example if potash is deficient in the soil then apples will be sweeter, but they will be smaller and less juicy at the same time. So where does quality lie? Is it in sweetness or juiciness? The decision is a personal one and each gardener must satisfy himself and so adjust his techniques and varieties to get what he wants from the soil.

It is true, however, that many modern plant varieties have admirable qualities of disease resistance and heavy cropping but in order to obtain heavy crops we have to add much artificial, usually nitrogenous fertiliser. If there is a lack of flavour in the variety then it is easy to blame the fertiliser and not the variety itself. Many people using the same variety, for example Golden Wonder potatoes, complain that the flavour has gone, but they are trying to compare maybe twenty years ago with today and one's memory is highly selective.

So there is no complete answer to the quality question, there are simply personal preferences, memories and maybe prejudices.

3

Using Manures, Fertilisers and Chemicals

Introduction

Of course, all substances are either simple or complex chemicals, but in this book, for the sake of simplicity, by *manures* I will mean bulky organic materials, by *fertilisers* I will mean simple chemicals containing essential plant foods, and *chemicals* will be used to indicate hormones, weed-killers with strange names such as 2-4-D 2-4-5-T and so on. Insecticides and fungicides, of which Derris dust and sulphur are probably the best-known examples, will be the subject of a separate chapter.

Manures

From time immemorial man has used manures to help feed his crops and, until the nineteenth century, the excreta of the cities was sold to farmers to put on the soil to enrich it. Because of this aura of antiquity manures have acquired a reputation which can be exaggerated although they are of vital importance to the soil.

Most manures are based on animal excreta usually mixed with straw or some other bulky material, but there are plenty of other types such as manures made of leather dust, spent mushroom compost, fish meal and seaweed. The quality they have in common is that they were once part of other living things and it is right to assume that they must contain the chemical substances which we associate with life. These chemical substances are based on nitrogen, phosphorus, and potassium in relatively large quantities, and a number of minor 'trace' elements such as boron, manganese and zinc. There is no doubt that plants can absorb very complex organic substances (are they not able to absorb weed-killers such as paraquat?), and they may absorb some of the complex substances undoubtedly present in manures. However, no real evidence to support this latter point has ever been adduced and talk of vitamins, enzymes and hormones being taken up by plants from manures remains more speculation than fact.

But even if green plants do not take up complex chemicals from manures, these substances are nevertheless present and so get into the soil where they are taken over by bacteria, used as food, and changed into much simpler chemicals which the plants can absorb. Still further properties are found in these complex organic substances because it is from them that the bacteria form humus, and many manures also contain groups of substances which will react with the soil particles and form them into good crumb structures. These substances are called *soil conditioners* and they are valuable, although once again their role in soil formation and structure can be overestimated.

Wise gardeners will therefore use manures for two reasons, firstly because they feed plants and secondly because they help to improve soil structure. A warning must, however, be inserted here for most manures are relatively poor in plant food as a glance at Table 1 will show, and they should be supplemented with chemical fertilisers. Also, many organic manures are attractive to soil organisms and gardeners may find the slug population has been increased by using vegetable refuse or even compost on the garden.

One great virtue of organic manures is that they are bulky and can therefore be spread over a large area in deepish layers. These layers will act as mulches or *weed smothers* before they are broken down to form plant food. The best organic manure is probably horse manure mixed with straw, but cow manure is very good and pig, goat and hen can all be used. Unless it has already been done the fresh manure should be mixed with straw or garden refuse in a compost heap and allowed to rot down before use. This generally takes about six months and

Table 1 Fertiliser Value of Organic Manures

Name of manure	% Nitrogen	% Potash	% Phosphate
Farmyard manure	0·6	0·6	0·3
Wood ash	—	10·0	3·0
Dried blood	12·00	1·00	1·00
Bone meal (steamed)	3·00	—	27·00
Compost (well-made)	2·00	1·00	0·75
Fish meal	9·00	1·00	10·00
Hoof and horn meal	14·00	—	2·00
Peat moss	1·00	0·2	0·1
Poultry manure (dry)	5·00	3·00	4·00
Seaweed (fresh)	0·3	1·5	—
Sewage sludge	3·00	0·2	1·00
Spent hops	3·50	0·3	1·3

allows most of the acids which it contains to be broken down. If this is not done, then these acids can damage plant roots and so reduce the ultimate value of the treatment.

But the best general advice is to use maximum quantities of organic material for on the whole it can do nothing but good. Before using it however make sure it is well rotted, and do not heap it around the base of plants and shrubs where it may hold moisture and set up rot.

Fertilisers

Many growers profess complete disdain for what they call 'bag-muck', but it is true to say that the crop yields which go to feed the millions of the world could not be obtained without the use of fertilisers. In fact there was a marked increase in the yield of all crops which coincided with the discovery of fertilisers in the latter half of the nineteenth century.

This revolution was based on the discovery that plants on the whole did not absorb complex organic substances in any quantity from the soil but were particularly dependent on three elements: nitrogen, phosphorus and potassium. Nitrogen, which they needed for leaf and protein formation, is in the form of nitrates or nitrites (NO_3 or NO_2). Potassium was absorbed simply as such and phosphorus as phosphates. Thus the whole diet of a plant could be expressed as NPK which are the chemical symbols for nitrogen, phosphorus and potassium respectively.

Later work has shown that plants need a much more varied diet than was at first believed and some thirteen different elements are necessary including, particularly, iron, magnesium, zinc, copper, sulphur, boron and molybdenum. These so-called 'trace' elements are only needed in very small quantities and there is usually enough of them in most soils or present as impurities in the ordinary grade of chemicals used as fertilisers. So it is only in chalk or limestone areas that the deficiency diseases caused by lack of trace elements have any real significance.

But the gardener really needs to know what fertilisers to use and the rule here is very simple. If you want to grow a leafy crop such as cabbages or lettuce or Brussels sprouts then ample supplies of nitrogen are necessary and these can be obtained from dressings of sulphate of ammonia or sodium nitrate. To grow good root crops, such as potatoes or beet, the soil must contain supplies of phosphate which can be given as superphosphates, and for seeds, for example peas and beans or fruit such as apples, the requirement is potash as sulphate of potash.

These are most easily supplied by using a compound fertiliser which contains all the major foods. There are many such compounds in which the proportion of the necessary elements is varied so that you can buy a compound potato fertiliser, or rose or tomato or lawn fertiliser, and these will do the job very well. Most bags of fertiliser have instructions regarding time and quantity of application but the easiest thing to remember is that plant food is only needed when the plant is growing, so it is a waste of money to appy, say, potato fertiliser in the autumn when the crop has virtually done all its growth. This means you should not apply fertiliser in the winter for there is little growth then and the rains will have washed it all away by the spring when the plants really need it.

It is always good husbandry to ensure that any seed bed contains phosphate either as bone-meal or super phosphates because nearly all the phosphate needed by the plant is taken in by the young seedling and a later application never produces such beneficial results.

So far as quantities are concerned, it is usually best to apply half the advised amount in the seed bed and when the plant is really growing well to give it the other half. Some fertilisers scorch the leaves if they adhere to them on a dry day and this is the reason why many fertilisers are granular for the granules roll off the leaves. It is nevertheless sensible to try to apply the material close to the ground and below the leaves or between the drills, preferably before a good shower of rain which will wash any fertiliser dust from the leaves.

Today one can buy 'slow-release' fertilisers. These are complete compounds which are so formulated that they dissolve slowly in the soil water and so are available to the plant over a long period of time. Such fertilisers rarely scorch but the slow-release carries an in-built disadvantage in that the fertiliser will carry on releasing its necessary foods all through the year and maybe even in the winter when there is little or no growth. They can therefore be wasteful if used, say, on beans which are only in the ground for ten to twelve weeks, but are very useful in a shrubbery or in plant pots where growth is taking place nearly all year round.

Most gardeners prefer to buy ready-made compound fertilisers but it is useful to know the values of these materials in terms of nitrogen, phosphorus and potash content. This is shown in Table 2 and if anyone wishes to experiment in mixing his own then the appropriate proportions can be mixed at home.

Table 2 Fertiliser Value of Chemical Fertilisers

Name of fertiliser	% Nitrogen	% Potash	% Phosphate
Growmore	7	7	7
Sulphate of ammonia	21	—	—
Superphosphate	—	20	—
Ammonium phosphate	21	—	61
Kainit	—	14	—
Muriate of potash	—	50	—
Nitrate of potash	13	40	—
Nitrate of soda	16	—	—

It is not necessary to buy trace elements, for many proprietary brands contain them already and if fertilisers are used to supplement organic manures then the trace element will be supplied by the manures.

Foliar feeds, designed for application to foliage, are being increasingly used for house or pot plants and these are simply mixtures of salts containing NPK along with some trace elements dissolved in water. The virtue of foliar feeding is the obvious one that, since the mixture is applied to the leaves, the plant can get a supply of food *before* the fertilising solution falls on the soil. Normally fertilisers are applied to the soil and this is perfectly satisfactory, but in lime or chalky soils reactions can occur which result in parts of the compound fertiliser being tied up chemically by the soil and so not being available for use by the plant. This can happen with boron and iron, and plants growing in these limestone soils may be unable to get iron from the soil because it has been chemically rendered insoluble. A foliar feed containing iron will allow this element to be absorbed by the leaves and so deficiency symptoms will not occur.

Alternatively special iron salts called chelates or sequestrenes can be applied to the soil. These are available to plants but are chemically inert so far as other soil chemicals are concerned. But limey or chalky soils are relatively unusual and need only trouble gardeners in areas such as Derbyshire or the Downs or in parts of Dorset.

Chemicals

A vast battery of different chemicals is being made available to the amateur gardener. They range from growth retardants, via bird repellents, total weed-killers, rooting hormones, fruit setting compounds to selective weed-killers and clearers of scum from ponds. It would be pointless to try to analyse them all in detail, but they have one thing in common, namely *they can all be dangerous*. This does not mean they should not be used, for every house is full of dangerous substances from paraffin and lighter fuel to aspirins, bleach and stain removers. What it does mean is that they should be used *only* according to instructions, they should be kept *in their own containers* away from children, and any container which has been used should be well washed each time after use as also should the hands of the user.

However, with this warning in mind, it would be a foolish gardener who did not use the methods and techniques of modern science to produce a better garden.

Weed-killers

Apart from fertilisers, weed-killers are probably more widely used than any other type of chemical. To use them sensibly it is important to understand the definition of a weed, namely 'a weed is a plant growing in the wrong place'. Note the distinction is made on the basis of *place* and *not* on the kind of plant. To drive this point home just consider that a potato plant in a grass lawn would be a weed but grass in a plot of potatoes would also be classed as weed.

The name weed-killer is therefore a misnomer, for they are all *plant* killers and it just happens that certain plant- or weed-killers can be useful.

Firstly some chemicals simply kill all plants. These are classed as total weed-killers and include such substances as sodium chlorate and paraquat. Sodium chlorate is very long-lasting in the soil and should only be used if you do not intend to grow plants in the treated area for maybe years. You can therefore use it on a path and it will be kept weed- (plant-) free for some years. But be careful of the water draining from the path for that will carry the deadly chemical along with it and may kill valuable plants some distance away. The other total killer is paraquat which, although deadly to many plants, is almost immediately destroyed or fixed in the soil and will not wash out or kill anything else. It attacks the green stems and leaves, so be sure you do not get any spray on valuable crops or plants for it is totally non-selective.

Another common weed-killer is simazine which is long-lasting in the soil and will kill seedlings as they emerge. It does not drain away like sodium chlorate nor does it disappear quickly like paraquat, so it is the ideal weed-killer for paths or for under shrubs such as laurels and even roses, but do not get it on the leaves of valuable plants and do not dig or hoe it in. It should be left where it falls on the top of the soil.

The other major group contains the selective weed-killers. There seems to be a touch of magic in these for by using them you can kill plantains on a lawn and leave the grass unharmed. This selectivity is a very valuable power with great potential which depends on the fact that simply because different types of plants *are* different, they react differently to certain chemicals. Human beings would be killed by many berries eaten by birds and in an analogous way brambles are killed by 2-4-5-T whereas grass is unharmed. The 2-4-5-T will also kill valuable shrubs and trees so that the weed-killer can only differentiate between broad-leaved plants which it kills and narrow-leaved plants such as grass which are unharmed.

Once again the best advice that can be given is to follow the instructions *exactly*. Don't be tempted into trying it a little stronger on the 'one-for-the-pot' principle and don't expect it to be any more selective than the instructions say it is.

Rooting hormones

The chemicals in the selective weed-killers are hormones which regulate or, in the case of the killed plants, which disorganise the regulation of plant growth. But hormones not only affect the rate of growth, they can also affect the kind of growth and can even stimulate new growth.

The rooting hormones do this last job for on a bare stem they can stimulate the development of roots, and so cuttings can be taken and rooted much more easily with than without their use. Of course, cuttings will root without the addition of these substances to the cut end, but they will root very much more slowly which means that they may dry out or be stricken with Botrytis rot before they can live on their own.

These substances are cheap and a small canister can be bought for a few pence. The savings can be enormous for by rooting cuttings obtained from friends you could populate a shrubbery for the cost of a packet of cigarettes.

The only advice needed for the amateur is to be satisfied with a little less than perfection. Not all your cuttings will root but the percentage 'take' can be increased by selecting the right type of hormone for the cuttings you want to root whether they are hardwood or softwood.

Common problems and queries

1. Can lime be used as a fertiliser?

Lime has practically no fertiliser value at all and the little it does contain (mainly calcium) can usually be obtained from humus or other soil particles. But lime is used a great deal for two main reasons. The first of these is to increase drainage because it improves the crumb structure of the soil and the second reason is to help alter the soil pH from very acid to much nearer neutrality. It is useful as an antidote to club root of Brassicas. This is a disease which attacks the roots of crops such as cauliflower, cabbage, swedes, Brussels sprouts and even wallflowers, producing large swellings or clubs which disrupt the life of the plant and may kill it. A good top dressing of hydrated lime, say 280 g/m^2 (8 oz/sq yd) along the drills, will not cure the disease but will reduce its severity.

Lime has another affect which is at the same time both useful and a nuisance. This results from the fact that lime will react with other soil chemicals and the effect of the reaction may be either to lock-up some soil chemicals, for example iron, so that plants can't get them, or the exact opposite in that lime may liberate many other chemicals such as nitrogen and potash. Part of the undoubted benefit of lime is certainly due to this release of plant foods, but of course soon the soil larder will be bare and need restocking. This means you must add the plant food fertilisers at heavier rates when you are using lime.

The point which then arises is when should lime be applied? The obvious answer is when it is needed and *only* then, and you can tell when it is needed if you use one of the soil testing kits sold widely by most garden centres. These are simple to use, will give you a sufficiently exact measurement of the pH of your soil, and if you buy one of the more complex but more expensive kits you will also obtain some idea of what fertilisers your soil lacks. Assuming lime is needed, how is it applied? It should always be applied to the soil surface in autumn or early winter and *never* at the same time as you apply your chemical fertilisers otherwise the chemical reactions described above may mean much of the fertiliser will be lost. There is no need to dig it in for the rain of the winter will take care of that but some lime scattered along the bottom of each spit as you dig will improve drainage in a very clay soil.

2. When is the best time to kill weeds?

The obvious answer is 'as soon as you see them'. This certainly applies to physical hoeing for weed seedlings die much more quickly if they are uprooted or disturbed than do mature weeds. The practical advice is to hoe in the morning when the young weeds will lie exposed to drying wind and maybe the heat of the sun all day. This will usually kill them, but if you hoe in the evening then the coolness of the night and the dew may be sufficient to give them a fresh start in life and you will be hoeing the same weeds the following week.

Many old gardening sayings have much good science in them and the one that comes to mind is 'one year's seeding means seven years' weeding'. This is accurate, for if a weed is allowed to flower and set seed then a single plant may produce some hundreds of seeds which will germinate in future years and give you no end of trouble. Seven years. . . .

The other approach to weeding is to use chemicals, and here the answer is not straightforward for it depends where the weeds are. If they are, say, in a rose bed then the careful application of paraquat or a hormone weed-killer at any time will do the trick. Be sure however that none of the spray gets on the leaves of the roses (or other desirable plants) or you may kill them too. Be sure you choose a still day to avoid drift to nearby plants. If the weeds are on a path, then it is best to use a complete weed-killer in early spring and with luck you will be clear all summer. But if the weeds are in a lawn and you have to use a selective weed-killer then a different treatment is necessary. Since selective weed-killers act by disrupting regular growth, they must be applied when weed growth is rapid. This may be May or June depending on your location but you will be able to tell easily for the grass will be growing quickly as well.

The ideal technique is to cut the lawn fairly short. Let it recover and the weeds and grass start growing again and before the grass has grown much apply the weed-killer according to directions. The weeds will die and, if the grass is growing well, it will fill in the space left by the dead weed and you will have no bare patches which could be recolonised by other weeds or by moss.

3. How and from what do I make a compost heap?
Compost can be made from nearly anything that has once lived. Admittedly materials such as peat or sawdust or old bones would be very slow to rot down, but household vegetable waste, fallen leaves, lawn mowings, any vegetable matter at all can be useful in a compost heap.

The essence of compost making is to create conditions which encourage the growth of soil bacteria, for as they grow they are changing dead organic material into compost. One must therefore be sure that the correct bacteria are present. These bacteria live in the soil and will almost certainly blow into the compost heap, but you can ensure their presence if you take care to sprinkle soil on the compost heap as it is being made, or you can cap the heap with a layer of soil.

There are a number of compost bins on the market made of plastic or metal, but the real compost enthusiast will only use natural materials, making the bin out of slatted rot-proofed wood. The bin must be of a reasonable size to allow the development of the high internal temperatures which should be obtained and about 60 cm x 60 cm (2 ft x 2 ft) is an easily managed size.

The vegetable waste should be put on bare earth (to allow earthworms, fungi and soil bacteria easy access to the heap) and allowed to accumulate until it is 15 cm (6 in) deep. The heap should not be too puffy but should be reasonably firm and com-

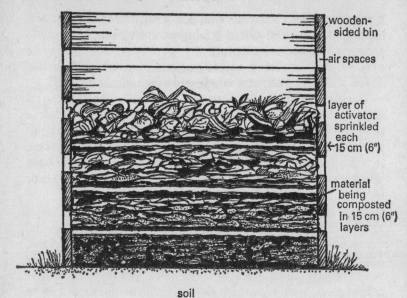

wooden-sided bin

air spaces

layer of activator sprinkled each ←15 cm (6″)

material being composted in 15 cm (6″) layers

soil

Figure 3 Formation of a compost heap. Note the sprinkling of activator every 15 cm (6in), and no base to compost heap.

pact. Many gardeners trample it down. Once a thickness of 15 cm (6 in) is reached then a source of nitrogen should be added to help the bacteria. This nitrogen is often called an *activator* and there are many proprietary activators on the market, but fish meal, dried poultry manure, even sulphate of ammonia will fulfil this function very adequately. Apply the activator at about 100 g/m² (3 oz/sq yd) and on top of it add another 15 cm (6 in) layer of vegetable matter, then more activator and maybe a sprinkling of soil to help increase the number of bacteria. Continue to add layers in this way.

The heap should be built to a manageable height and then finally capped with a 5 cm (2in) layer of soil or a plastic sheet or even an old carpet. The cap will stop the heap from becoming absolutely sodden in a wet winter. The compost will take six to twelve months to mature and when perfectly made will be a brown powder in which it is impossible to identify the materials you put in. Even if you don't reach this height of perfection, the material can still be used, for the decomposition process will continue in the soil.

If you are short of vegetable matter to make compost, then a bale of straw, preferably wheat straw, can be used to bulk up each layer of the heap.

In a perfect compost heap, the high temperature will kill weed seeds, diseases and insect pests, but the beginner in compost making should avoid putting diseased material on the heap, for if the disease spores are not killed then the compost would simply spread the diseases all over the garden when it was used.

4

Stems and Roots

Roots

If you were going to build a tall structure with a narrow base you would certainly have problems in getting it to stand upright. These problems would be greater if the top was very heavy, irregularly-shaped and exposed to the full force of the wind. To solve these problems, and a look at any telegraph pole confirms this, you sink the base in the ground and you have a series of guy ropes to hold the structure vertical. You might even sink the base in a concrete block to give additional weight at the foot and then you could have a fairly stable structure.

As plants and especially trees developed they were faced with a very similar problem, for, as we shall soon see, all plants need light and air and the only way to ensure that light reaches all parts of the structure is to make it either tall and thin, or flat and thin. But the other requirement of 'air' effectively rules out the flat thin answer, for this sort of structure would only have the *top* surface exposed to the air, unless, and it is a very important unless, you combine both ideas and have tall thin structures bearing flat thin extensions. So as plants (which are our 'structures') became taller and bore leaves (which are our flat thin structures) then the need for firm anchorage became very important. Thus root systems were evolved and it is the roots which support the plant, giving it a firm hold, resistant to very high wind pressures.

But roots have other functions and since many of these are

important to gardeners they are worth discussing in a little more detail.

(a) Roots as anchoring organs

Everyone who has pulled up a weed knows, although he may not recognise the fact, that the plant has at least two kinds of root. There is often a *tap root* which plunges deep down into the earth and there is a mass of so-called *fibrous roots* which are always near the surface and which mean that you often pull up quite a clod of earth along with the weed. Some plants have both types of root, others just have one or the other, but good examples of fibrous roots are the clumps of grass you may weed from your path or rose bed, and many of our most persistent weeds such as dandelions have a deep strong tap root.

To carry our analogy of the tree/telegraph pole a bit further, the tap root gives the deep solid support provided by sinking the pole in the ground, while the fibrous roots are the guy ropes,

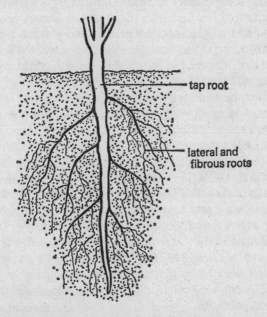

Figure 4 A simple root system.

except in this case they are underground guys. Usually short-lived annual weeds have only fibrous roots for they are not exposed to high winds nor are they very tall. It is the perennial weeds which come up year after year which have the deep tap roots. These not only serve as anchorage, but are also used by the plants as a place in which to store food especially in the winter.

It is for this reason that simply to hoe the top off a thistle or a dandelion is almost useless, for there is enough stored food in the tap root to allow the plant to grow a new top and carry on as if nothing had really happened. Thus to kill difficult perennial weeds it is best to use chemicals which will penetrate to the tips of the roots, or to hoe the top off regularly in the hope that you will eventually exhaust the food stored in the tap root and the weed will die.

Apart from anchorage and storage the tap root has no other function and it is the *fibrous* roots which are the feeding roots and which the gardener must attend to very carefully. If you try to untangle the base of a plant and its fibrous root system you will find that the roots are not only very extensive, spreading out from the shoot, but also that they vary in thickness being strongest near the tap root and thinnest furthest away from the plant. What this means is that the oldest part of a root is nearest the plant and the new actively growing part is at its tip.

It is easy to mark roots and see where and how they grow, and observations of this type demonstrate two very important things for the gardener. Firstly, the growing tips are very fine and delicate and are therefore easily damaged by stones or hard pieces of soil which they meet as they grow. This is most likely to occur in the seedling stage when roots are very tender indeed and when the plant is too young to withstand any damage to its roots. It is obviously therefore of vital importance to make sure that seed-beds are in a nice fine crumbly state which is easy for the roots to penetrate. Seed-beds should contain no stones.

The second point is that since the root system as it grows spreads out from the main plant, it is pointless simply to put fertiliser close to the base of the stem for the mass of the roots is not there. You should always therefore apply food a little way away from the stem. This is not so important in the case of a small annual plant which will not have a very extensive root system, but it *is* important in the case of fruit trees and bushes. In fact it is often said that in feeding fruit trees such as apples or pears, the fertilisers should be applied to the soil around the *drip-line*. The drip line is an imaginary circle where water would drip off the tips of the branches if you imagine the fruit tree as a big umbrella.

(b) Roots as feeding organs

The fact that roots are part of the feeding system of the plant is general knowledge and it has already been assumed above, but there is a lot more to roots and feeding than the problem of 'where to feed', for roots also absorb water from the soil in vast quantities and any lack of water in the soil is speedily shown by the plant wilting and maybe dying.

The first question to answer is how the plant gets water and food from the soil. If the young part of the root is examined it will be seen to be covered with very fine hairs called *root hairs*

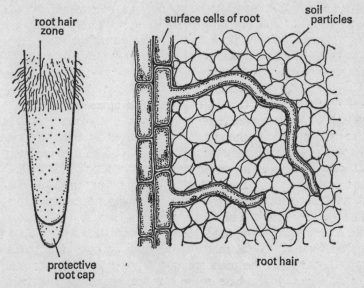

Figure 5   Root hairs in the soil.

45

and it is this very delicate and fine mass of hairs which act as the actual feeding pathways.

A root hair is not a solid structure but is hollow, like a minute tube. Each of these tubes leads into the fine roots which in their turn lead to coarser roots and so into the rest of the plant. There is therefore a passageway through which food and water can pass from root hairs right up to the top of the tallest tree, and the main difficulty in conceiving how plants feed is understand-

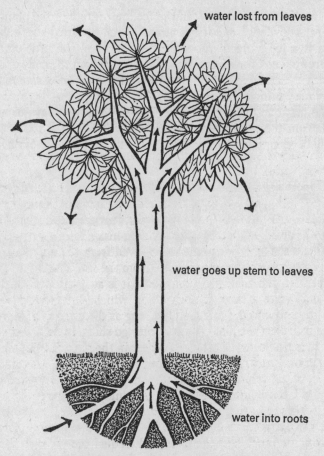

water lost from leaves

water goes up stem to leaves

water into roots

Figure 6   The path of water in a tree.

ing the mechanism for the actual movement of water and food from the soil, through the root hair wall and so into the general system of the plant.

There has always been controversy about how water moves in a plant and particularly how it gets from the soil up to the top of a giant tree. There are three mechanisms all of which may be in use at the same time, or they may act singly. Firstly, water may move up the plant by capillary action which is the force shown by water as it is soaked up by blotting paper. The second force is that exerted by a pump, and many scientists think that roots may exert a pumping action inside the plant although this is hard to demonstrate. The third force is a simple pull up by the leaves as they lose water. This must not be confused with suction, for water can only be sucked up 9.6 m (32 ft) and most trees are higher than that, but it is a real pull which, because the water is in fine threads in the xylem (q.v.) of the tree, is absorbed by the water column as if it were a solid wire.

There may be other forces at work but the general result is that water will flow into the root hair and be lost by evaporation from the leaves.

It has already been said that the root hair is very small and so, since it is a hollow tube, the wall must be very thin indeed. This is so, and not only is the wall thin, it is also saturated with water. Therefore, if water is taken from inside the root hair and passed up the tube, the water is removed from the wall, which will in its turn extract more water from the soil.

Although the analogy is not exact, it is as if the wall of the root hair were a kind of wick along which water could pass from the soil into the plant, and so long as there is lots of water in the soil, then the plant should never go short. In reality there may be a temporary shortage of water in the plant if it is losing water more quickly than it is getting it from the soil. This situation is called *temporary wilting* and rarely does any serious harm. It is seen quite often in house plants where watering has been neglected or forgotten, but temporary wilting is much less cause for alarm than overwatering. In fact many more plants die from too much water in the soil than die from too little. The best watering system for most house plants is to let them get to the stage of wilting and then give them a good soak, unless you have a soil moisture meter which can give you accurate information about the condition of the soil.

Water has many important properties and we will be concerned with some of them later, but the one of interest at the moment is its ability to dissolve salts of many kinds. Some of these are salts which contain nitrogen, phosphorus and potassium, essential to the life of the plant, and it used to be assumed that as the root hairs took in water, the essential foods were passively carried along into the plant. This is now known to be untrue, for if it were true it would mean that those plants which took in the most water would contain the most salts, and measurements and experiments of many kinds have shown the simple explanation to be a fallacy.

The reality is much more subtle, for it has been shown that root hairs are *selective* in what they absorb from the soil and they may reject some chemicals altogether and allow others in in such quantities that they became economically valuable. A good example of this is a seaweed which will absorb iodine from sea water (where it is present in very small quantities) and accumulate it to such an extent that it is commercially feasible to extract it. Similarly a plant may grow in a soil rich in lime and only allow in small quantities necessary for its growth.

But if a root hair is selective and can keep some chemicals out and others in then it must use some *energy* to carry out this selective task. The energy used by roots is derived by a chemical reaction which uses oxygen, as the energy in coal is released as heat if it is burned in the presence of oxygen. Roots therefore need oxygen if they are to function properly.

In the chapter on soil it was pointed out that a flooded soil contained no oxygen and a dry soil contained no water, and that therefore a good garden soil should contain a nice balance of water and air. This is most easily achieved if the soil is rich in humus, which allows water to be stored in the humus without blocking up the air passages between the soil crumbs.

It is well worth remembering that roots demand a different diet from that needed by leaves, and in particular they need quantities of phosphate. This is especially true in the young seedling stage and every seed-bed, or seed box for that matter, should be given a sprinkling of superphosphates at about 35 g/m² (1 oz/yd²) to ensure a good start in life for all your seedlings.

Gardeners tend to pay attention to the stem and leaves and flowers of their crops and forget about the roots, the hidden providers, simply because they are hidden underground, but from what has been said a few further important gardening conclusions can be drawn. For example, since the fibrous feeding roots are near the surface where they have easy access to water and oxygen, it is pointless to bury a lot of plant food deeply in the soil, for the roots won't be able to use it. Organic matter, compost and dung can be buried where it will rot or be spread by worms so improving soil texture and drainage, but never put artificial fertilisers deeper than 22.5 cm (9 in). It is best to sprinkle these on the surface and let the rain wash them to the feeding roots where both food and water will be available at the same time.

Another conclusion is that roots near the soil surface will have ample supplies of oxygen but could be in danger of dying back following a spell of hot weather. This is one of the great virtues of mulching with compost, straw, or some organic-rich substance which will form a cool and moist layer and provide what gardeners call a *cool root run* even on the hottest days. Mulching is especially valuable for climbers or shrubs grown against a wall because the soil is often thin and impoverished in that kind of situation and a good mulching around the base of a clematis or even a climbing rose will help to keep the plant in good health.

Stems

When we talk of plants we practically always mean stems and leaves which collectively are called the *shoot*, and although they should not be separated in one's thinking, for the sake of convenience they will be treated separately. First, however, it is important to look closely at the point where a leaf joins a stem.

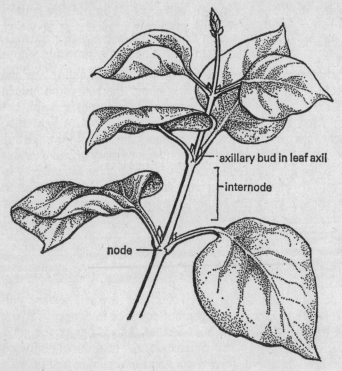

Figure 7 Leafy stem, growing nodes, internodes, leaf axils, and axillary buds.

This junction is called a *node*, the length of stem between nodes is called the *internode*, and the angle at which the leaf (or the leaf stalk) enters the stem is the leaf *axil*.

We are tempted to call any flat green expanse a leaf, but there are flat green stems, and round green leaves which look like stems, and the precise definition of a leaf is important. It is 'a (usually) flat green structure which bears a bud in its axil', and if this *axillary bud* is not present we may be dealing with a leaf-let, or a pinnule, or even a stem, but we are not dealing with a leaf.

Nearly all branches of trees and tall annuals are really the result of the growth of the axillary bud, and if you look carefully at the base of a very young branch you can often see the scar which was left when the leaf fell off. Here we have one of the nice bits of growth regulation found in plants, for the axillary bud is controlled by two forces. The first is the leaf in whose axil the bud is found, for normally the bud cannot grow until the leaf has been removed either by nature or by man. This is because the leaf produces a substance which inhibits the growth of its own axillary bud.

The second control is exerted by the tip of the shoot which bears the leaf and so the bud, for the tip also produces this inhibition and prevents the growth of buds lower down the stem. These two facts are closely bound up with many gardening practices which make sense when they are understood. Take, for example, the pruning of hedges and fruit trees. In the case of the hedge, one of the reasons for trimming is to reduce the height, to keep the hedge under control, but another is to make the hedge denser and thicker.

The reason is that trimming the hedge cuts off the tips of the

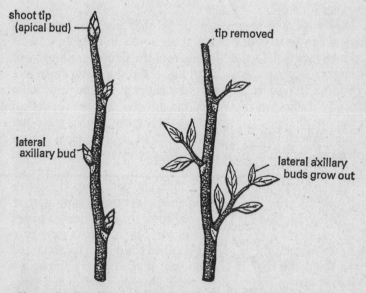

Figure 8 The effect of removing the tip (apical bud) of a shoot.

stems so that the axillary buds are no longer inhibited and grow out, thus thickening the hedge. The old saying that 'growth follows the knife' simply points to the fact that if you cut off one branch tip you may remove the inhibition on six or seven buds all of which will grow. This simply means that instead of one branch you now have six or seven. The same principle applies in pruning fruit trees. If this is done injudiciously, you may end up with a thicket of thin twigs, so if you prune be sure you leave two or three buds at most, or better still don't prune unless you have good reason.

The upward growth of the young tip will of course increase its distance from the buds at the base of the stem which will start to grow in succession as the tip grows upward. Hence most plants are basically pyramidal or conical in shape.

It may be good practice to remove axillary buds as they develop, for example, in tomatoes or chrysanthemums, for if they were retained their vegetative growth might make the fruit or flower crop much later in maturing and in a bad year you could get no crop at all. So the junction of stem and leaf has an importance of its own.

The stem can be regarded as the 'bit that bears the leaves' and the leaf can be regarded as the 'thing borne on the stem'. Stems can take many and varied forms from the slender twining stem of bindweed to the vast solid trunks of oaks or Californian redwood. But in essence stems are the pathways through which a two-way traffic goes on. Water and mineral salts are carried up to the tips of stems and branches where growth takes place and to the leaves, while food manufactured by the leaves passes down the stem to be used to provide energy for the plant or as storage food during the winter.

This two-way traffic follows different paths, for the water and mineral salts pass up through the central woody part of the stem while the manufactured food from the leaves passes down the stem via the bark. Of course both these pathways have technical names, the wood being called the *xylem* (pronounced *zylem*) and the bark is the *phloem*. It is also very important to know that in plants whose stems live for more than a year, for example a fruit tree, there is a thin layer of tissue called

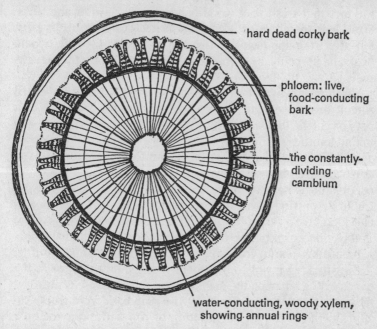

hard dead corky bark

phloem: live,
food-conducting
bark·

the constantly-
dividing·
cambium

water-conducting, woody xylem,
showing· annual rings·

Figure 9   Cross-section of the stem of a young tree. In order to
show it clearly the thickness of the cambium has been exaggerated.

the *cambium* which separates the xylem and phloem and which
has the remarkable power of producing more xylem and phloem
each year. It is this annual production of new tissues which
allows us to count the number of annual rings and so tell the
age of the tree.

Some horticultural techniques are based on this knowledge.
Many unfortunate gardeners have discovered that rabbits
have a liking for bark (phloem) and gnaw it away all round the
stem or trunk. Of course this effectively stops the downward
passage of food to the roots which die and so the tree is killed.
When this happens the tree is said to be *girdled* and it is an old
foresters' way of killing trees before they were felled.

(As a kind of postscript, in the vast teak forests of Burma the
trees were always girdled and left to stand dead for two or three
years before they were felled. The reason for this was based on

T.Y.B.O.G.—4

the fact that fresh teak wood is heavier than water and sinks. Fresh logs therefore could not be floated downstream in rafts, but after standing dead for two to three years the trees would float and so could be transported down the rivers to the saw-mills.)

Girdling however need not be total and a variation called *ringing* or *ring-barking* is sometimes used in orchards. This consists of cutting out a thin strip of bark half round the tree and taking another strip round the other half of the tree but about 15 cm (6 in) lower or higher. Food can therefore move up and down the tree but the movement is slower because the transport channels have to dodge around the cuts. It is like slowing traffic by putting two barriers halfway across the road as at a check-point. So far as the tree is concerned the food moves so slowly that parts of the tree are slightly starved and the consequence may be to force the tree into flowering and fruiting.

Ring-barking is not to be generally recommended, for in the hands of the amateur the damage may be too severe or diseases may get in the wound. Vandals who strip bark from trees usually kill them. A simpler variation of ring-barking is to use a pruning knife and instead of taking out a strip of bark simply to make a fairly deep cut round half the tree with a similar one above. The interruption in food supply may be enough to starve a reluctant fruit tree into fruiting.

The xylem is the water-conducting tissue and it is largely composed of dead cells which act almost as tiny pipes through which the sap flows. Because the cells are dead they can have little or no resistance to disease especially those types of diseases caused by wood-rotting fungi. This means that when a branch is cut off, as in pruning, an unprotected surface is exposed which consists largely of dead xylem surrounded by its ring of phloem. Very often food materials will ooze out of the phloem and xylem and these provide a good source of food for the spores of fungi which float everywhere in the air. Some of these will be wood-rotters. An examination of trees will often show that rots have gained access to the trunk via a pruning wound and the life of the tree may be drastically curtailed thereby.

All pruning wounds should therefore be painted with a protective coat of pitch, creosote, or one of many proprietary paints which contain fungicides and are specially formulated to do this job well.

But it is the properties of the cambium, that thin layer which lies between the xylem and phloem, that give rise to some of the most important gardening techniques. To make this point clear remember that the cambium layer, by continuous multiplication of its cells, keeps on producing xylem and phloem, in some cases for hundreds of years. It is an area of rapid cell division and its products in the beginning are almost the simplest form of plant cell—it is as they age that these cells begin to change into a mature form, such as xylem. If two areas of cambium are brought into contact, each of them carries on dividing and producing new tissues, but slowly the new cells from the two cambiums begin to intermingle and in the end it is very difficult to separate them. In fact if they are left in contact long enough for the new cells to change into xylem (wood) and phloem then the result of this intermingling will be that the two cambiums and the wood they produced are joined together.

This is the basis of grafting, which is used very widely in many plants such as apples, pears, lilacs and rhododendrons in order to tailor the shrub to an almost exact requirement. In the case of the apple, the technique is as follows. A *rootstock* is selected for the variety. These rootstocks are produced in the main at the Research Station at East Malling and are given names and numbers. Thus we have Malling 9 (IX) or Malling 17 (XVII), each with its peculiar properties. Malling IX is known as a *dwarfing* stock because it develops a very poor root system.

Having chosen the rootstock we then select the variety we would like to grow, for example Cox's Orange Pippin. A plant of Malling IX with a stem about the thickness of a lead pencil has its top cut off with a slanting cut at about ground level. This top can then be rooted like a cutting and used again, but it is the stump and the roots which are used for the graft. A twig of Cox's Orange Pippin of the same thickness as the Malling IX stem is then selected and a clear slanting cut made at its base.

55

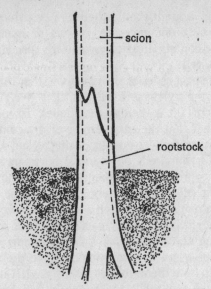

Figure 10   A grafted plant. Note the cambiums are in contact at the graft point.

It is possible then to fit the twig (*the scion*) to the rootstock exactly and tie it firmly in place.

What has been done is to bring the cambiums of the Malling IX and the Cox's together and they will grow, multiply and eventually form a tight union at this graft point. The advantage now gained is that the Cox's Orange Pippin will not be growing on its own roots but on the poor root system of the Malling IX. The resultant Cox tree will therefore be small and will come into fruit in five to seven years. By comparison, if a vigorous rootstock had been used this might have produced a tree 6–9 m (20–30 ft) high which bore no fruit for twenty years.

By varying the subjects of the graft, different types of the same plant can be produced, the only limitation being that the stock and the scion must be closely related. Thus you can graft apple/apple and pear/pear but apple/pear will not 'take'.

A similar technique is the process of *budding*, in which instead of using a twig as a scion, a bud of the scion is inserted into the stem of the rootstock, again making sure that the cambiums are in contact. When the bud has 'taken' and begun to grow you simply cut off the plant of the rootstock down to the bud you wish to preserve and it will grow on as a single plant. Practically all hybrid tea and floribunda roses are the result of this technique, the rootstock being a common hedgerow briar and the scion buds being of the desired variety. In the case of roses, however, the briar rootstock is vigorous and so the garden roses are much larger and more productive of flowers than if they were on their own roots.

There are still further horticultural properties inherent in stems. One of the most important arises from the fact that not only do stems have buds in the leaf axil, but they also have many areas of cells which can be stimulated to grow by a number of different means. Injury is a very common stimulus, and just as we form scar tissue when injured so does a plant. If a branch is sawn from a tree obviously quite a serious injury is produced, not only to the cambium but to the rest of the trunk and especially the phloem.

If pruning wounds are watched over a long period of time a certain sequence of events always occurs. Firstly a kind of skin of cork forms over the edges of the wound where the phloem and cambium are situated. This is followed by rapid growth and the result is a raised area around the edges of the wound of what is called *callus tissue*. Given enough time this tissue will heal over the wound and it is to provide the time that we paint wounds. By painting the wounds we provide a seal which keeps out fungus infection, and in some paints there are chemicals which will speed up the callus formation and heal the wound more quickly.

The wound of course is not one-sided for if there is a pruning wound on the trunk, there must be a similar wound at the base of the branch which was sawn off, and as you would expect the same sequence of events should happen here. There is one important difference, however, for the branch being no longer attached to the tree has no water or food supply and so usually dies.

But, even if only twigs are cut off, a wound will still be

produced and the wound reaction will take place. The twigs can then be put in the ground where the callus tissue will form and from this tissue roots will be produced which will begin to supply the twig with water and mineral salts. In other words we have taken a 'cutting'.

Cuttings can be taken from most plants for the process described is almost universal in plants, although in a number of cases, for example azaleas, it can be very slow, whereas in willows or geraniums it can be rapid. Remember that cuttings have no water supply until they are rooted, so they should be kept in a moist but not saturated environment to prevent excessive loss of water and death by desiccation.

Finally some stems run along or under the ground as *stolons* or *rhizomes*. These bear axillary and other buds and often these will be stimulated to grow by injury caused by hoeing or weeding. In fact many of the most troublesome weeds, such as ground elder, couch grass and creeping dock, owe their success to the frequency with which these usually dormant buds begin to grow if damaged. If you try to hoe out ground elder you will simply break up the underground stem causing multiple wounds and so provide the stimulus for many fresh buds to grow. Such weeds may be treated chemically but where this is impracticable the only alternative is to dig out *every* piece. You must get it all out for it is said that 'every bit with two ends will produce at least one new plant!'

Leaves

Leaves come in many guises, the grass we cut and the lettuce or cabbage we eat, the simple shape of an elm leaf or the complex and intricate tracery of a fern leaf, the tiny scales of a broom or the huge umbrella-like leaves of bergenia. But the shape and even the size doesn't really matter for all leaves have the same function, namely to manufacture food for the plant. Of course leaves may do other jobs as well. They can be protective as in holly or nettles, they may attract insects as in poinsettia or begonia and they may be used for storing water, as is the case in many succulents and cacti, but all these other functions are secondary to the primary one of feeding the plant through a complex series of chemical reactions called *photosynthesis*.

There is no necessity for the gardener to understand the chemistry of photosynthesis. Books have been written about it and there's still a lot to be learned, but the basic facts are so simple that anyone can grasp them. This is not useless knowledge but of real significance to any grower, for the leaves feed the plant, and so particular care should be given to provide the best possible conditions for this process. The word photosynthesis is derived from the Greek words 'photo' meaning 'light' and 'synthesis' meaning 'putting together'. Essentially therefore photosynthesis is 'putting together using light'.

The easiest way to explain the process is to look at its beginning and its end and to forget (nearly) the long complex chain in the middle. The beginning is the simple chemicals carbon dioxide (CO_2) and water (H_2O) and the end is a bewildering range of complex organic substances such as sugar ($C_6H_{12}O_6$), starches, fats and cellulose. If in ordinary life we try to join things together we have to use energy. For example if we simply tie two bits of string together we have used our own energy in making the knot, if we use a screw and screwdriver, or solder, or mortar, or anything to link two separate things together, energy is needed.

Put simply, photosynthesis links CO_2 and H_2O together and by linking *this* combination to other things, complex organic substances are produced. This needs energy and it is supplied by light, usually sunlight. Of course the world has lots of water in rivers, seas and lakes, and the air is full of carbon dioxide, so you may wonder why photosynthesis does not take place everywhere. The answer is that the energy in sunlight can only be set free and used by the green colouring matter in plants known as *chlorophyll*.

Photosynthesis then can be written as a kind of chemical equation in which one side shows CO_2, H_2O, sunlight and chlorophyll, and the other side of the equation shows the finished product as follows :

$$CO_2 + H_2O + \text{Sunlight} + \text{Chlorophyll} \rightarrow \text{Starches, sugars, fats etc.}$$
$$\text{(energy)}$$

How can this knowledge be used to make things grow better?

If the process is analysed, it breaks down obviously into the four components on the left-hand side of the equation. It is wrong to think of them separately since all are necessary at the same time, but it is much simpler to do so and we can add the complexity later if necessary.

(*a*) *Carbon dioxide* (CO_2)

Although there is only .03% CO_2 in the air, there is such a vast quantity of air that the supply of CO_2 is virtually inexhaustible. The reason for the inexhaustibility is that, as fast as plants take CO_2 from the air and change it to, say, sugars, we or some other animals, or even bacteria, eat the sugars, change them back to CO_2 and H_2O and breathe them back into the air again. To use a current word, CO_2 is continually *recycled* and so can never be all used up. But although this is true and the CO_2 keeps being returned to the air, situations may arise in which there can be temporary CO_2 shortages and the most common of these is in the greenhouse or cold frame. Imagine a greenhouse full of tomato plants on a nice sunny day. The tomatoes will all be photosynthesising like mad, using up CO_2, and unless there is a good supply of air to replace the CO_2 the rate of photosynthesis can slow down. It should be clear then that as well as keeping the greenhouse or frame cool, adequate ventilation is necessary to ensure that CO_2 supplies are always adequate. It is dangerously simple to assume that the air contains the best concentration of CO_2 for photosynthesis. This need not be so and it can be proved that in a controlled situation, such as a greenhouse, considerable increases in crop can be obtained by artificially piping CO_2 into the greenhouse.

But in the garden outside there is little we can do to increase CO_2 concentration so we have to try to make the best of the other factors.

(b) *Water (H_2O)*

Of course this refers to water at the roots which will be transported up the plant to the leaves where it will be used in the photosynthetic process. Soil water supply has already been discussed in Chapter 2 and so, other than to stress once more the value of humus in the soil to keep it moist, water need not be further discussed here.

(c) *Sunlight*

Light is a form of energy and what photosynthesis does, viewed from another angle, is to change light energy into the chemical energy which is locked up in the variety of compounds which is produced. In the case of man this chemical energy can be released when we digest food and may appear as heat energy, in almost exactly the same way as the chemical energy in coal or wood is released as heat when we burn it. In fact, photosynthesis, if we look at it closely, is not so much concerned with chemicals and their changes, as with the ways in which energy from the sun is made to flow into our bodies and those of every other living thing.

Looked at from this angle the question of light becomes paramount. Most gardeners know that plants need light and within limits the more they get, the better they grow. This means that shady places should be avoided as far as possible, and sources of shade, such as overhanging trees and high hedges, should be eliminated if this can be done without spoiling the attraction of the garden.

Fortunately most plants can use fairly weak light so that they will survive in shady conditions, but they will not be able to photosynthesise effectively and so will be unable to produce much excess food for storage. Many of our vegetables are eaten for the stored food they contain, for example, potatoes, carrots, turnips and parsnips, and anyone who has tried to grow any of these in the shade knows that the tops may be quite tall and green but the tubers or roots will be woefully thin and may even be totally worthless as food.

There are many plants however which can carry on photosynthesis even in rather dim light and such plants are often found in woodlands or even as house plants in rooms where little daylight will penetrate. You only have to think of *Aspidistra, rhoicissus*, many ferns and even *Ficus elastica*, the india-rubber plant, to realise that by appropriate choice of species or variety, you can grow plants almost anywhere. The critical point, however, is that shade-loving plants, such as ivies, very rarely produce flowers in any quantity and almost never will they produce fruits or even edible parts.

(d) Chlorophyll

This is an almost universal pigment found in all green plants whether they be mosses, ferns, seaweeds or cereals. There are a few minor variations from the main structure of chlorophyll, but generally it is found in structures named *chloroplasts* which are shaped rather like tiny thickish discs.

It is a surprising thought that chlorophyll changes light energy into chemical energy, but it itself is entirely dependent on light for its formation. If a plant is grown in total darkness it will not be green but yellow and immediately it is exposed to light it will green up as the yellow pigment is changed to chlorophyll. This is another reason why good light is necessary, for without it not only is the rate and amount of photosynthesis reduced but the actual production of chlorophyll may be hampered.

The chief cause of a reduction in chlorophyll content and therefore of the efficiency of the plant is, however, a shortage of certain elements in the soil. By growing plants in the absence of nitrogen, iron, magnesium or even boron it can be seen that there is a marked yellow colour to the leaves instead of the healthy green of chlorophyll. Usually the shortage of nitrogen can be overcome by supplying a good fertiliser to the plant, but the deficiency of iron or boron is more difficult to cure. This is because it occurs in chalk or limestone soils which react chemically with many metals, and to cure these mineral deficiencies in such a soil demands the application of special chelated compounds or foliar feeds or humus or all three (See Chapter 2).

Another cause of lack of chlorophyll is virus disease, which often shows up as smaller mottled yellow leaves, and if this type of disease is suspected, the good gardener will simply pull out and burn affected plants.

There is also a hereditary lack of chlorophyll which can be shown in some plants as yellow or even white edges to the leaves, for example as in tradescantia and some ivies, or the whole leaf can be yellowish, as for example in golden privet. Any plants with yellow or variegated leaves are usually less efficient than normal green plants and so grow more slowly and less profusely. If, therefore, in a golden privet an ordinary green shoot appears, then it is wise to cut it out at once or it may eventually swamp the more decorative branches and cause them to die out. Similar advice applies to all variegated forms such as ivies, hollies, and aucuba.

Transpiration

Every leaf is continuously losing water by evaporation. This process is known as transpiration. It may be at a great rate, as on a windy hot day or it may drop to virtually nil as on a rainy night. Water evaporates through the surface of the leaf in much the same way as clothes on a line will dry, or it is lost through the millions of pores in the leaf surface, the *stomata*. Each stoma is not just a simple hole in the surface, but has two guard cells, one on each side, which can open and close the pore and so regulate water loss.

The regulation by the guard cells is largely in response to light and is associated with photosynthesis. Carbon dioxide gets into the leaf through the open stomata and as CO_2 goes in so water vapour can evaporate out. But at night when there is no light energy available for photosynthesis it would be dangerous to the plant if it lost water all the time, so the guard cell mechanism causes the cells to shut in the dark and open in the light.

The processs of transpiration has two possible benefits to the plant for as the water moves from the root up to the leaf in the transpiration stream it carries with it salts from the soil to help feed the plant. Probably as important is the fact that when

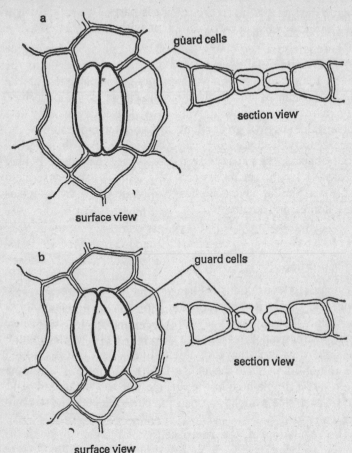

Figure 11 Stoma: (*a*) closed and (*b*) open. Note that the opening is controlled by the guard cells.

water evaporates it uses up heat so that transpiring leaves feel cool even on a very hot day, and this process may protect many plants from sun scorch.

Finally if you hold a leaf up to the light you can see the network of veins which is necessary to move water and food in and out of the leaf. This network connects to the main vein and then to the stem, branch, and eventually trunk in a tree and right down to the root hairs in the soil. It is part of a complete system supplying every part of the plant with great efficiency.

Common problems and queries

1. *How dangerous to buildings are the roots of plants?*
The roots of plants will very rarely cause a building to fall down but they can certainly cause indirect damage to property. Such damage can arise very simply from leaves blocking gutters, or from the roots of trees getting into leaking drains and blocking them completely. This is very common, especially if it is a slightly leaking sewer, for the water will then contain plant foods and the tiny roots will penetrate fine cracks, and as they grow will maybe burst the cracks still more widely.

A much more serious, although less common, cause of damage occurs in clay soils, for clay expands when wet and contracts when dry. In a dry summer the roots of a tree can extract great volumes of water from a clay soil. This can cause sufficient shrinkage to open up soil cracks and the foundations of a wall may lose support and the building suffer in consequence.

As the total volume of roots gets bigger and bigger, a sideways pressure may be exerted if they are confined, say, by the wall of a garden on one side and by the wall of the house on the other. The garden wall quite often breaks with the pressure and may spill on to the road. Many gardeners will have seen a pot bursting as it gets too full of roots.

Shrubs are almost harmless in this connection but trees should never be planted close to the house.

2. *I have read of 'root nodules'; what are they?*
Root nodules are swellings commonly found on the roots of peas, beans, lupins and most members of the Leguminoseae family. They are caused by the presence in the root of millions of bacteria which locally stimulate the root to grow hence the swellings. They are not restricted to the pea family and similar nodules can be found on alder roots and a few other plants.

The bacteria in the roots take nitrogen from the air and pass it to the plant so that the relationship helps plant growth. Such bacteria will also help to enrich the soil and many gardeners do not pull peas and beans out of the ground once the crop has been taken, but rather cut them off at ground level, leaving the nitrogen-rich roots in the soil to benefit further crops.

3. What is the reason for pruning in winter?

Of course one doesn't always prune in winter, and spring-flowering shrubs should be pruned as soon as they finish flowering in late spring. This allows them lots of time in the summer to form new flower buds for the following spring.

Many shrubs and trees however are pruned in winter and the main reason is that it is easier to do then, for you can see the tree without the hindrance of masses of foliage. The framework of branches will stand out and so it is simpler to shape the tree correctly. Leaves can be heavy things and the pieces of branch which have been sawn or cut off are easier to move and burn than if they were thickly furnished with leaves.

In addition the shrubs/trees are usually dormant, so that a wound will not interrupt the flow of water and nutrients so dramatically in winter as it might were the tree under considerable growth stress in the summer.

4. Do sprays damage a leaf at all?

The obvious answer is that it depends what you spray with, but that is much too glib. It is always important to follow the maker's advice very carefully, for many sprays against insect or fungi are toxic in high concentrations but quite safe at the advised levels. It is sometimes wondered if sprays will block up the stomata and so stop photosynthesis. Once again this is very unlikely and although there is evidence that sprays can affect some functions such as transpiration, normally any damage done is much less than the loss which could follow if you did not spray.

There are plastic films that can be sprayed on shrubs or trees which are being transplanted which do reduce transpiration (they are called anti-transpirants) but this is a good thing for it prevents excessive loss of water from the leaves when the roots are out of the ground or have not yet become established. The film breaks down in a week or so and the plant resumes normal life.

5. *We eat leafy vegetables such as cabbage and lettuce. How should they be fed?*

All plants need a complete fertiliser but certain plants are more demanding of some substances than others. The usual advice given is that for vegetative growth—and that generally means leaves or stems—the element in greatest demand is nitrogen. This is often supplied as sulphate of ammonia or an organic substance such as fish meal or dried blood, but the majority of ordinary gardeners use compound fertilisers such as Growmore which contain all three vital substances, nitrogen, phosphorus and potassium. But it is the proportions of these three which then becomes important. The most common ratio is probably 7:7:7 which means seven parts each of nitrogen (N), phosphorus (P) and potassium (K). For a leafy crop it may be possible to get a high nitrogen compound fertiliser which would be 15:7:7 or some other mixture in which more than one third (7/21) is nitrogen.

5

Flowers, Fruits and Seeds

Introduction

In general botanical terms the root, stem and leaves are known as the *vegetative* parts of the plant and the flowers, fruits and seeds as the *reproductive* parts of the plant. These definitions are not strictly true because it is possible to multiply plants using vegetative parts only, for example from tubers or bulbs or cuttings. Nevertheless if a gardener is going to try his hand at plant breeding and hybridising then he must use the reproductive parts, for only there is there a sexual process, and the evolutionary function of the reproductive parts is to ensure the development of further generations.

Because the reproductive parts are so essential, in fact they are absolutely vital, to the continued existence of flowering plants, it can be said that, once evolution had developed the basic structure of the flower, there has been very little departure from it. True there are variations in colour, size, shape and even the way in which flowers are borne, but these are simply frills on an established structure and all flowers are constructed on the same plan.

Flowers

The essence of sexual reproduction is the fusion of a male cell with a female cell, for by this process different qualities and characteristics can be brought together from each side and blended in a new combination of qualities. Flowers therefore

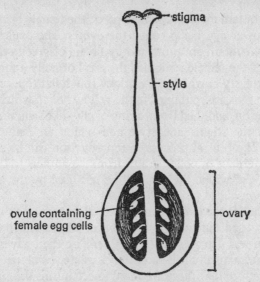

Figure 12 A vertical section of a hypothetical flower.

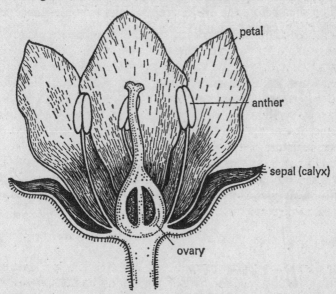

Figure 13 The enlarged ovary of a simple flower to show ovules, stigma and style.

usually contain male and female parts, the female being central to the flower and being called the *ovules*. The ovules and the eggs they contain are protected by layers of green cells and at the top of the female structure there is normally a longish projection (the *style*) which has a sticky rough flat top, the *stigma*. The male cells are contained in the yellow *pollen* which is normally borne on, and shed from, a ring of club-like structures which surround the stigma and style and which are known as the *anthers*. The central process in reproduction can be said to be the transference of pollen grains from the anthers to the stigma as a result of which the ova will be fertilised by the male cells and seed produced.

If further evolution is to take place and new and strange combinations tried out against the environment then it would be very pointless if plants could only fertilise themselves, for this would automatically rule out new character combinations. One finds therefore that there are many mechanisms to prevent this happening. For example, in some flowers the anther is ripe and pollen shed before the ovules are ripe, and in consequence self-fertilisation cannot occur.

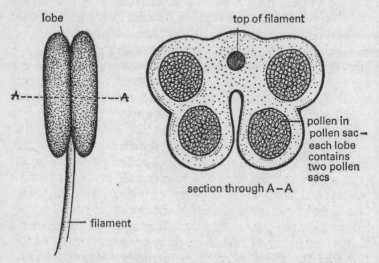

Figure 14   A typical anther and a cross-section of it.

Other plants produce flowers which are essentially one-sexed because either the anthers or the ovules are sterile. In other cases plants only bear male flowers and other plants only female flowers (many hollies are of this kind and it is a bit of a shock to realise that Silver King holly is all female and Silver Queen all male!). All sorts of means are used and the most effective and widespread is a biochemical barrier which ensures that pollen from any given plant cannot cause fertilisation of its own ovules.

This is not to say that self-fertilisation does not occur, for it does, and some of our best fruits are self-fertile as are runner beans, but self-fertilisation is the exception, and where fruit and seed form the crop, for example in apples, care has to be taken that compatible inter-fertile trees are planted or there may be no crop at all. Since self-fertility is the exception and since it is disadvantageous from an evolutionary standpoint, the flowering plants were faced with the problem of getting the pollen of one plant to the stigma and style of a similar plant some distance away. There are two almost universal transport systems available to plants, namely wind and water. Each of these could carry pollen along and *by chance* could deposit it on the stigma of a similar plant some distance away. Notice the use of the words 'by chance' for it would be a stroke of good luck if the correct pollen got to the correct stigma.

Nevertheless, this method of air-borne pollen seems to have been the first successful method tried by nature and many very important plants are fertilised in this way. Probably the most important group of plants in the world, namely the grasses to which all our cereal crops belong, are wind-fertilised. So also are the willows, pines and many others.

This method however has two great disadvantages, of which the first is that it is very wasteful of pollen. For every pollen grain which fertilises the correct plant, millions of grains must be lost by landing on other plants, on buildings, in the sea, in fact anywhere other than on the appropriate stigma. To solve this problem the grasses simply produce masses of pollen over a long period in dry weather. Every hay-fever sufferer knows this fact well, for as the pollen count increases so does his misery.

We can say therefore that wind-pollination is very uneconomic in terms of the energy the plant must put into the production of pollen.

Another difficulty with wind pollination is the problem of getting the pollen into the open air where it can be blown about. This is often done by having anthers which dangle outside the flower as in the grasses. When the wind blows it shakes the pollen grains out as if they were grains of pepper from a pepper-pot. At the receiving end the style and the stigma of a wind-pollinated flower are often long and feathery so that the wind will blow not only round but also through the stigmatic area and the correct pollen will stick there. Grasses often have such feathery stigmas and pussy-willow catkins are in fact the silvery felt-like hairs of the stigmas.

But nature came up with a much better idea and it is not entirely a matter of chance that the rise of the flowering plants to their present dominant position took place at the same time as the rise of the insect world, for there has developed a very close and mutually advantageous association of insect and plant. This association shows itself by the plant using the insect as a carrier of pollen and in return providing it with food such as nectar.

To return to the structure of the flower, everyone grows them in the garden mainly because they are beautiful, brightly col-oured, with interesting shapes and scents. All this attractive colourfulness lies in the two circles of organs borne outside the anthers. These are the *petals* and the *sepals* (or calyx). Since the petals are the best-known part of a flower, they can be used to make the appropriate points, but it should always be remem-bered that in many cases the outermost ring of floral parts may be a dull green and simply protective (a rose bud), but in other flowers (the daffodil) it can be as brightly coloured and attractive as the petals and often not distinguishable from them.

Insects have a reasonable sense of colour vision and it can be shown that they will be attracted to flowers of a particular colour at a given time. Thus they do not expend energy explor-ing leaves or walls but can fly straight to the flower. In finding the flower they are helped by the scent and often there are markings on the petals which almost indicate a landing-strip.

At the base of the petals on the stigma there are frequently glands which secrete nectar, so the insect pushes its tongue down to the nectar and in so doing will rub against the anthers which deposit pollen on its back. The insect will then fly to another similar flower and this time as well as getting nectar it will deposit some of the pollen from its back on the stigma of the second flower. This ensures cross-pollination.

From this simple routine plants have evolved elaborate mech-isms to ensure that the insect lands at the correct place, deposits the pollen it carries on the stigma and goes off carrying a fresh load. These mechanisms range from lever-type stigmas which bend to touch the insect's back as it lands, to elaborately-shaped flowers which mimic the shape of, for example, a bee. Another bee will then come and try to mate with the imitation and will thus effect pollination.

The structure and function of flowers is a strange and fascinating world and every gardener should take time to sit and watch insects at work among his flowers as by so doing he will add a new dimension to his gardening interests.

On the practical side, however, many gardeners get much interest and pleasure from crossing their own plants in the hope of obtaining a new and better variety. Many of our best roses, sweet-peas, carnations and so on, have been bred by amateurs, and no-one can start this hobby without a knowledge of floral structure. There are books on this subject but two considerations are paramount. You must prevent self-fertilisation in a flower you want to cross and stop air-borne pollen from another variety of the same species interfering with your cross and producing misleading results. The first problem can only be solved by gently opening the bud before the pollen is ready to be shed, and plucking out the anthers with a pair of fine tweezers. This emasculates the flower and ensures that self-fertilisation will not occur. To make sure no foreign pollen gets at the flower, you enclose it in a small muslin bag to keep out insects and any wind-borne pollen.

When the time comes you then take pollen on a soft brush

from the flower you wish to cross to the emasculated flower, and there you deposit it on the stigma. The muslin bag is then retied and there follows the period of waiting to see if your technique has been good and seed is produced.

Seed

As stated above, seeds are the result of the fertilisation of an ovum by a pollen cell, but the fully developed seed is a far cry from the fertilised cell, for a number of new tissues are now formed, some from the parent mother plant to form the fruit, and others from the fertilised cell itself to form the complex structure we call a seed.

With a certain degree of elaboration all seeds have three basic parts, a protective seed coat, a food store, and the embryo plant itself.

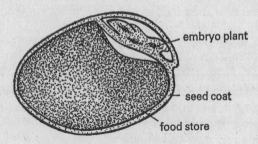

Figure 15   Section of a seed.

The seed coat is the layer which naturally first meets the eye and when examined in detail it is found to be a fairly tough, nearly waterproof layer, so that when we eat seeds, such as peas and beans, it is the seed coat which we may find difficult to chew. The main function of the seed coat is protective and many of them become thick and hard as in a sweet-pea.

The seed needs protection because it has a few serious enemies of which the most prevalent are the soil bacteria and fungi. Given full rein they would treat the seed like any other organic material and fairly quickly reduce it to humus. The other major enemy is animals who may swallow the seed in their food. There it could be digested by the stomach acids and enzymes were it not for the seed coat.

But because the seed coat is protective, keeping out all hostile organisms, it naturally acts to keep in the contents of the seed. Thus a perfect tough seed coat would let no water or air pass in or out and would maybe stop the young embryo plant from getting access to the soil and so begin to grow. This difficulty is resolved rather neatly for each seed coat bears a tiny hole through which water can pass slowly. The food store is rather like a chemical sponge which soaks up water from the soil and this movement of water into the seed precedes any active growth. The absorbed water increases the volume of the stored food which can be seen to swell and in so doing can usually burst the seed coat. This allows much more water in and so the process of *germination* can begin.

Of course, if the seed coat is very thick and tough, the force with which the water is drawn in to the seed may not be enough to rupture the seed coat, in which case a kind of stalemate ensues with the food store trying to draw water in and the tough coat allowing no room for the increase in size of its contents.

Many hard-coated seeds, of which sweet-peas and clover are good examples, sometimes prove very difficult to germinate, and gardeners who are worried by this problem will deliberately weaken the seed coat by nicking it with a knife, or by rubbing it between sheets of sand paper or even by chewing it for a number of hours so allowing saliva to soften the coat.

Under natural conditions, if hard-coated seeds are sown, the coat is attacked by soil micro-organisms which eventually weaken it and allow germination, but this is a hit-or-miss business and some seeds may lie dormant in the soil for years before they can germinate. However, it must be said immediately that tales of wheat seeds germinating after some 2,000 years in Egyptian tombs have been very conclusively disproved.

Another result of the hard seed coat is that gas cannot pass through. This may not seem very important until it is realised that seeds, rather like us, take in oxygen and give off carbon dioxide. But carbon dioxide cannot escape through the seed coat so it tends to accumulate and one of the main consequences of CO_2 accumulation is that life slows down nearly to a stop. Here therefore is another reason for the long life of many seeds, for they exist at a very low level in a state of prolonged dormancy until the seed coat breaks and the gases are released.

In order for the embryo plant to grow and develop roots and shoots it requires energy and this is supplied by the stored food. In most seeds the storage food is starch (wheat, rice) but many other seeds contain quite high quantities of protein (beans, peas), and other seeds fats and oils (linseed, sunflower). But these storage foods have to be used in a variety of chemical reactions to release the energy and the materials needed for growth. If it is put in another way, the stored food has to be used to provide both the energy and the materials for the new roots, stems and so on which are necessary to allow the embryo plant to reach the surface and manufacture food by photosynthesis.

To change stored food to anything demands chemical change, and chemical changes will only take place if the temperature is high enough. In addition a large number of the chemical changes which are part of the germination process demand oxygen in fairly large quantities. It is in fact a relatively simple matter to make a list of the things which are absolutely necessary if a seed is going to germinate. These must be provided in the seed-bed or the seed will just lie there and eventually be destroyed by bacteria and fungi. The necessary factors are:

(1) Water
(2) Oxygen
(3) A reasonable temperature

The ideal seed-bed should therefore be made of open, humus-rich soil which will drain fairly quickly and so allow oxygen in, and seed should not be sown in it until a temperature of 45°F (approx. 7°C) can be maintained. Seed composts should contain about equal quantities of peat and sand and, as mentioned in Chapter 3, a little superphosphate to help root development. Some seeds have special requirements such as light, but these are very much the exception and, in general, gardeners will be little worried by this problem.

An important consequence arises from the size of the food

store, which is approximately the same size as the seed. On this store the life of the new plant will depend until it reaches the surface and can look after itself. The depth at which the seed is planted then becomes of great importance, for small seeds, if planted too deeply, will not contain sufficient food to allow the new plant to reach the surface before the food runs out. The seedling therefore dies. Similarly if a large seed is planted too shallowly it may not have access to enough water in its vicinity to allow proper swelling and so bursting of the seed coat.

Depth of planting is therefore vital to the gardener and a rough rule of thumb says that normally seeds should be planted at a depth of not less than once or more than twice their own diameter.

Finally we come to the third part of the seed, the embryo. This is the essential part for, using appropriate techniques, one can grow embryos without seed coats or food supplies, but we cannot grow seed coats or food supplies into new plants. An embryo starts out as one cell which is the result of the fusion of the male and female reproductive cells, but it rapidly begins to grow and, as the rest of the seed develops around it, it becomes possible to pick out the young root and the young shoot. By the time the seed is ready to be shed from the parent plant, the root and shoot are clearly delineated and, once shed, if the seed get the right conditions, they will grow.

There are exceptions to this which are important and one of these is the case of seed which is shed before the embryo is ready to grow. This kind of seed will then require a period of time to become fully mature before germination will occur and a number of seeds, such as holly and rose, are of this type. In other cases, the embryo is so ready to grow that, unless the seed is sown right away, the embryo will begin either to die or will go into a state of dormancy that takes a long time to pass. Into this category falls the seed of a number of polyanthus and primula varieties.

The purpose of seed is to ensure the continued existence of the plant species and to do this the seed has to be shed into the ground where it will germinate and grow. Thus seed *dispersal* as it is called could be achieved quite easily simply by letting the

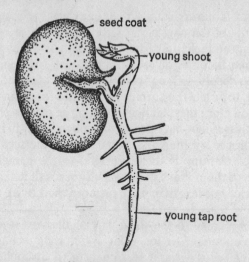

seed coat

young shoot

young tap root

Note: burst seed coat

Figure 16 A germinating bean. Note that the young root is the most advanced structure and the shoot is much smaller.

plant or the flower die, for the seed would then simply fall off. In a few cases this happens but such a process has a few built-in disadvantages, for the seed would tend to fall around the parent plant and the young seedlings would have to grow in soil which might have been exhausted by the parent, or even in the shade of the mother plant if it were a perennial.

Another disadvantage would be that all the seeds from the same plant would fall in roughly the same place where they would compete with each other in such a way that none would get off to a good start. Further if seed distribution were as limited as this, any given area would become crowded with the same type of plant and any pests or diseases which attacked them would have a field day. By the same token the spread of the species would be limited and very slow so that it would rarely be exposed to varied types of environment and the process of evolution would slow down.

The flowering plants have largely overcome this seed dispersal problem by having evolved many and varied devices to distribute the seed. Some, such as dandelion or sycamore, developed parachuted or winged seed which can float long disances in the air. Poppies have developed a type of pepper-pot mechanism which shakes out seeds in the wind, while broom and lupins have a kind of catapult system of rapidly twisting the pods as they burst which can throw the seed some distance. But in most cases the dissemination of seeds is associated with the *fruit* and so it is appropriate to consider this part of the plant now.

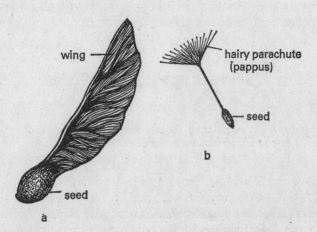

Figure 17   Wind-dispersed seeds (*a*) sycamore; (*b*) dandelion.

Fruit

To most lay-men a fruit is something juicy which you can eat such as an apple, strawberry or orange, and these *are* truly fruits, but to a botanist a fruit is a very definite plant structure which sometimes has, but more often has not, anything to do with food and pleasure. If the definition of a fruit is put in non-technical terms it could be said to be 'part of the parent plant formed after pollination which has the role of protecting and helping to disseminate the seed which it contains'.

Under natural conditions all fruits contain seeds and this category includes such diverse objects as a pea-pod, a hazel-nut, a blackberry, and of course all the ordinary things called 'fruit'. It must be pointed out that some cultivated fruits do not contain seeds and in fact seedless bananas, grapes, grapefruit and so on are very important articles of commerce. The reason for this apparent exception to the definition is that man has learned how to trick the plants by allowing them to be pollinated, which sets up the fruit-forming reaction in the mother plant, but using pollen which cannot fuse with the ova and so no seeds are formed. It has even gone so far that we can use fruit-setting chemicals which will carry the pollination stimulus without any pollen being used and so there are no seeds.

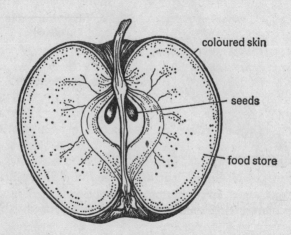

Figure 18 Section through an apple, a typical juicy fruit.

Generally speaking, however, all fruits contain seeds and it is part of the science of fruit growing to be sure that if you are only planting one fruit tree you make sure that it is a self-fertile variety such as Victoria plum, Conference pear, or James Grieve apple. If you want two or more varieties in order to have an eater and a cooker, or say, an early and a late maturing apple, then the choice of varieties can be all-important. For a list of compatible varieties which will produce good fruit you are advised to consult *Growing Fruit* by Roy Genders in this series.

Fruits are very important agents of seed dispersal for many

fruits are succulent and are eaten by animals. Berries are very obvious in this connection and gardeners see their berberis and pyracantha stripped by birds which eat the berries for the food they contain. Because the seeds have a protective seed coat they are not killed during the digestive processes and are excreted by the birds maybe miles away from the site of the parent plant. Other fruits are covered with hooks and spines (such as teasel, cleavers) which become entangled in the fur or fleece of an animal, carried away by it and then get rubbed off or actually fall off during a moult, so spreading the species. Man of course is probably the greatest culprit in this connection. He can travel very long distances in a very short time and either intentionally or by accident has spread his crops and his weeds all over the world. Thus it is very often said that one of the best signs of human habitation in the past is the presence of large clumps of nettles today.

Because the fruit is bigger than the seed and encloses it, it can act as a thick protective coat during hard icy winters, and some fruits will actually keep the seeds they contain totally dormant until the fruit is destroyed by bacteria or fungi. Only when this has happened will the seed germinate.

The colours of fruits are very noticeable, and if you make a list of brightly coloured fruits it will be found that practically all of them are eaten by animals. It seems as if the fruit advertises its presence to the bird, or small mammal, simply in order to be sure that it will be eaten.

Common problems and queries

1. Do all plants have flowers?
All plants which bear flowers are classified together under the name angiosperms, and all other plants including conifers, mosses, ferns, horsetails, fungi and seaweeds have other methods of reproduction usually by some form of spore not borne in a flower. But every plant, be it ever so humble, has, or has had at one time some form of sexual process in which a male cell fuses with a female cell. A good example of the loss of sexual function is often seen in some modern potato varieties which

never flower at all. Clearly they cannot reproduce by seed, but since potatoes are propagated by tubers, seed is unnecessary and could in fact be a disadvantage.

Because plants have this marvellous faculty of being able to be propagated by cuttings, tubers, bulbs and in many other ways, the ability to seed is not essential in many cases. In some situations where the flower may be pollinated by any other flower of the same species (not necessarily the same variety) the seed which might be produced would not breed true. If roses are taken as an example, a rose bed of mixed colours and varieties would be impossible to maintain if they had to be propagated by seed. Since roses are propagated by buds this problem never occurs and the rose breeder has to go to considerable trouble to force many modern rose varieties to produce fertile pollen and ova, much less produce viable and true seed.

2. What are F1 hybrids?

If two different varieties of any plant are crossed the resultant offspring are known as *hybrids* (note that they must be different varieties). It was discovered that if a variety was self-fertilised (inbred) for many generations the eventual plants were all very similar and you then had an inbred line, but if you produced inbred lines of two varieties and then crossed these inbred lines, the resultant hybrids were not only very much alike but they tended to be bigger, more brightly coloured, higher yielding than either of the parents. This type of hybrid is known as an F1 hybrid where 'F1' means the first generation.

If you then inbreed the F1 hybrids the result is an F2 hybrid which is less desirable than the F1, and if you continue to inbreed such a hybrid the vigorous good qualities are rapidly lost. For this reason gardeners are not recommended to keep the seed from an F1 hybrid, and new F1 seed should be bought each year. Because the two parents have to be kept separately and then crossed each year, the seed of F1 hybrids are usually more expensive than that of ordinary varieties, but the resultant crops are so markedly superior and very often earlier than the true varieties that commercial growers and those who show professionally usually prefer them.

Cuttings from F1 hybrids will show the hybrid vigour of the parent but since most F1 hybrids are annuals, cuttings are very rarely of any value. Efforts are now being made to produce F1 hybrid perennials, shrubs and trees and when these are freely available it may be a feasible proposition to propagate these vegetatively.

3. If I collect seed from my own garden, what techniques should I adopt?

Many gardeners get great interest and pleasure from saving the seed from their own plants and then growing it on the following year. The techniques necessary are very simple for the only real pitfall is dampness. If unripe seed is collected it will usually contain quite a high percentage of water and if it is stored in this condition it will go mouldy and the embryo will die. Seed should only be collected when fully ripe and this can be judged when the plant sheds it naturally. If it is shed on the ground the seed may be lost, so when you have selected the flower from which seed will be collected, enclose it in a muslin bag (to allow air in and out) and simply wait until the seed is shed into the bag. Of course if you are dealing with a plant such as an apple or even raspberry you wait until the fruit is ripe, or even over-ripe, before you collect it.

Once the seed has been collected, it must be labelled (or things will get mixed up) and spread out to dry in a temperate dry room, and when it is judged to be absolutely dry it should be bagged, preferably in foil-lined paper to keep out moisture.

The conditions of storage are vital for if moisture is available the seeds will absorb it and start to speed up their life processes which can also hasten their death. For the same reason mould spores will start to grow on the seed itself and many moulds produce toxic substances which can completely kill the embryo. Both the mould and the seed prefer a moderate temperature to grow well and it is in your interest therefore to keep the storage room as cold as possible so long as you avoid real frost.

The recipe for success is therefore made up of two elements, dryness and coolness, and as long as you stick to these you won't go far wrong.

4. I have heard of flowering being controlled by light. How is this done?

Many plants will only flower if there is a given length of day, but others such as daisies and many other weeds, will flower in any day length and are known as *day neutral flowers*. Chrysanthemums will not flower in a day-length of more than twelve hours and are therefore classified as *short-day* plants, while many summer flowerers are *long-day* plants and demand a day length of *more* than twelve hours. The phenomenon is called *photoperiodicity*.

Generally speaking this need not bother the ordinary gardener to any extent, but this knowledge is used a great deal by professionals who prevent short-day plants (chrysanthemums) from flowering by giving them additional periods of light and only providing the correct day length when the market is seeking these flowers. On the other hand long-day flowers can be prevented from flowering by using shades which artificially shorten the day.

It is not generally known that it is the leaves which sense the day-length by means of coloured chemicals known as *phytochromes*. These chemicals are changed by light, and in long days a lot of the chemicals are changed from one form into another whereas in short days only a little is changed. It is the balance between the unchanged and the changed substances which directs the plants to flower or not.

In reality the process is more complex than has been stated for in fact it is the length of the night which is significant and not the length of the day, but since our understanding is only very rudimentary at the moment it may be some time before the full implications and significance of this process can be worked out.

5. Does the rootstock or the pollinating variety of an apple affect its flavour?

The apple which we eat is formed from the parent tree, and although the formation of the fruit is triggered off by the pollen, the pollen only has a part in producing the seed. The flavour of the fruit is entirely dependent on the stock which bears it. Thus a Cox's Orange Pippin will always taste the same irrespective of whether it is grown on a dwarfing stock or on a fully-sized stock. The same reply can be given about the role of the pollen-donating variety which also has no effect on fruit flavour.

6

Pests and Diseases

Introduction

In thinking about pests and diseases it is important to get things into perspective. There *are* a large number of pests and diseases which could affect your roses, potatoes and other plants, and if they really got going and were left to wreak their havoc freely, they could reduce or maybe destroy the plants. But, and it is a very big but, they very rarely do so and the average gardener will find that in his garden there will be a few troubles which can give him serious problems but the majority of diseases and pests will simply pass by and be hardly noticed.

Further, plants are very tough things with great powers of recovery, so that, for example, roses can come back from a bad attack of mildew and still give you a worthwhile show. Another aspect of the strength of plants is shown by their inherent resistance to many infections especially if they are grown well and given ample food in a good soil. In fact it is sometimes said that a well-grown plant will not take disease or be attacked by pests. This is extremely doubtful and it would be more true if one said that a well-grown plant will give you a good crop *in spite* of disease and pests. So an immediate moral is obvious, namely give your crops the best possible conditions.

Another side of the general problem of loss due to pests and disease is the increasing emphasis being placed on methods of control by chemicals and in other ways. These will be discussed in more detail later in this chapter but they are mentioned at this point to show that even if some affliction strikes your plants, all need not be lost since many products of the chemist and the plant scientist can come to your aid.

Finally, this introduction is not intended to be a guide to the identification of pests and diseases on all garden plants or to tell you how to control them, for that would be a book in itself. Rather it is intended to show how there are basic principles which underlie the prevention of disease, and if these principles are applied carefully and with intelligent foresight, many problems would either vanish overnight or would maybe never appear at all.

Pests

There are pests of all kinds varying in size from rabbits and birds down to tiny insects which attack plants, but the usual working definition of a pest is an animal whose feeding reduces either the aesthetic value, or the economic value of the crop. Heavy grazing of trees by elephants could come under the heading of pest damage, but in the average garden this is a *very* rare occurrence, so for purposes of simplicity only the problems set by insects will be considered in this section.

There has always been a close connection between plants and insects. It has been shown that plants form the basic food of all living organisms either directly or indirectly, and in the case of insect pests the relationship is very direct. Thus we can see cabbage or gooseberry bushes stripped of their leaves by caterpillars or sawfly, we can see rose buds covered with greenfly and cauliflowers wilting from attack by cabbage root fly. We immediately recognise insect damage of this kind, but we don't often realise that our sickly yellow dahlias or raspberries are being attacked by virus diseases which are often spread by aphids. So the damage can also be indirect. This close connection is part of the natural balance which seesaws over the years. Insects will eat the crop until there is so little crop left that the insects begin to die of starvation. There will then be few insects left so the crop will begin to grow better and then later the insect population will build up again. Thus a balance is sustained.

For the gardener and the farmer such a balance is of no use

at all, for he wants good flowers and fruit and vegetables every year and not just in a 'seesawing' fashion. As a result he tries to reduce the swing of the seesaw by pest control and so ensure a steady level of production.

Another point is very often overlooked by those who are re-acting against a 'controlled' environment and chemical foods and who seek very sincerely for a return to Nature with a capi-tal 'N', namely that gardening is a completely artificial system of plant production. Nature never planted a row of cabbages or an acre of potatoes. The crops we grow, the sweet-peas, Brus-sels sprouts, in fact all our garden plants, are man-made. So much so that but for man and his technological advances they would not exist and certainly many of them could not continue to exist.

Thus to talk about a return to Nature is nonsense if carried to an absolute degree, but there is the opposite danger that if we neglect to remember that plants are living things and not little machines, we may stray so far from nature's seesaw that we do harm by our over-enthusiasm.

To control the pests of the garden, therefore, we have to try to understand their life histories and their ways of living. There is an old maxim in the field of plant protection which has very wide application but is often forgotten by the beginner: 'you must attack your enemy when he is at his weakest and in the smallest numbers'. In pest control therefore when is any pest at its weakest?

The weakest time is usually in the egg stage when the insect is static and cannot fly or run away from us. This, in our climate, usually means in the winter and the egg is the method used by many insects to withstand ice, snow and cold winds. This there-fore means that winter is the time to wash down and clean greenhouse and cold frame, to collect fallen debris such as twigs and leaves and burn them and, in the case of perennials and trees and shrubs, to apply a good winter wash containing substances specially designed to kill eggs.

If we take the other half of the maxim about 'the smallest numbers', then the obvious time to attack is at the beginning of the season, usually the spring, when pests such as greenfly have come through a hard winter, many have died, and those that remain are weak. A good dosing with a greenfly killer would save a lot of work and maybe heartache in the summer by when their numbers would have multiplied many times if left alone.

Another aspect of pest control allied to 'weakest' and 'fewest' is 'where is the pest to be found'? As a boy I remember a riddle which used to produce paroxysms of laughter. It was 'Where do flies go in the winter time?' The answer was 'Into the glass works to make blue bottles'. Not very funny, but it holds the great truth that in the winter time you may not find the flies, or the caterpillars, or the greenfly, or the red spider in their usual places. This is more obviously so if we remember that many of our crops, such as peas, lettuce and annual flowers are out of the ground and away by the late autumn. So, where *do* pests go in the winter time?

There are really only two answers to the query. The first is 'they go to plants which are still growing', the so-called *weed-hosts*. Thus blackfly on beans will spend the winter on the spindle tree (euonymus). Many greenfly will move to hawthorn hedges or grasses and so on. Thus a weedy garden has every chance of being a pest-ridden garden and as soon as a crop of, say, cabbage is finished it should be pulled out of the ground and put on the compost heap. Good efficient garden hygiene practised each autumn can go a long way to reducing the load of pests.

The second answer to the query is 'they go into protected places where they will be sheltered from the worst of the weather'. Such protected places may be very obvious, such as under the staging in a cold greenhouse, or into the rough cracks in the bark of an old apple tree. For other insects protection may be in the soil or under stones or inside canes for flower-staking, and the great shelter for pests of climbing plants is in the narrow space between the plants and their support. So in winter you should untie vines or climbing roses and spray the wall behind them; winter wash should not only go on the leafless fruit trees and bushes but also on the soil around their base.

Careful observation of the spread of our insect pests shows that the pest is first seen near its over-wintering site, then as the weather improves it multiplies and spreads until the whole plant and usually adjacent plants are all infested with the pest. The best advice is to treat early before the pest is serious. You may wonder how you can treat a pest if you haven't seen it. The answer is simple, for what you had last year you are likely to have this year and the next and the next, so treat your garden as if last year's pests were still there.

One of the main reasons for the great success of the insect world is its amazing reproductive capacity. For example in his book *Insect Natural History* (Fontana, New Naturalist, 1973) Imms tells us that a female aphid can produce about fifty young. In eight to ten days each of these will produce fifty young, so that at the end of a season roughly thirteen generations would have been produced and the total number of aphids would be $(50)^{12}$. This is an astronomical number and luckily disease, other insects and the weather, greatly reduce these numbers, but the problem of a rapid build up can be very clearly seen. $1 \times 50 = 50$; each of the fifty have fifty young in eight days : $50 \times 50 = 2,500$; each of the 2,500 have fifty young in eight days : $2,500 \times 50 = 125,000$; $125,000 \times 50 = 6,250,000$ in thirty-two days. In forty days the number is 312,500,000. A further eight days would yield more aphids than there are people in all of China, India and Russia put together.

Such figures from one overwintering aphid emphasize the necessity for an early start to control, but it also means continued control all through the summer. Many beginners feel that once they have sprayed against a particular pest or disease all will be well, and it would be if every insect were killed and if none blew in from next door. But nobody 'gets' them all and they do blow in from hedges, fields, weeds, next door and many other places, so that a regular spraying schedule against pests is good sense, and even if there are no pests, it is at worst a very good insurance policy.

Diseases

Although the distinction between pests and diseases is fairly clear cut, there are enough similarities between them for everything said above to be applicable to disease also. What is a disease? It is exactly the same as a pest except that the causal agent is not an animal such as an insect, but is a plant such as a *fungus* or a *bacterium* or a *virus*. A number of quite important plant diseases are caused by the presence or absence of chemicals such as iron in the soil (see Chapter 2) but for our purpose, the term disease will be restricted to fungus or virus infections.

Nearly everyone has a fairly clear picture of an insect in their mind, but very few people can picture a fungus and still fewer a virus. The simplest possible picture of a fungus is one of a large number of very fine threads of living matter. These threads may be separate and form a filmy layer on or in a plant and an example of this is mildew. In some cases the threads may be woven together to form a compact mass such as a toadstool or mushroom. When we get down to the size of bacteria we are moving into the microscopic. Although we think of bacteria mainly in terms of the diseases they cause to man, such as whooping cough, peritonitis and pneumonia, they are essential to the continued existence of life on this planet, for it is bacteria which are the main agents of decay allowing all the food locked up in living things to be released into the soil and reused, again and again. The appearance of a virus is very simple as most plant viruses look like tiny grains of sugar or tiny pieces of string. It is important to get an idea of the scale of size of a virus for they are small enough to cause diseases and even the death of bacteria. In fact they are so small and simple that the argument about whether they are alive or non-living has always depended on how you define 'living'.

In all three cases, however, the significant fact is that neither fungi, viruses or bacteria can manufacture their own food and are absolutely dependent on outside sources of food supply. We are therefore concerned with those fungi which have living plants as their outside source of food. In taking food from the plant they set up symptoms which we call disease symptoms and which may in the end lead to the death of the plant.

The most obvious symptom produced by many fungi is a thin greyish film on the outside of the plant, usually on a leaf or a green stem. This film of fungal threads penetrates some distance into the plant to tap its food supplies and by the general public such diseases are named *mildews*. There are many types of mildew caused by many different fungi, but probably the most common is rose mildew, or in some places gooseberry mildew.

Another group of fungi set up symptoms which appear as discoloured spots or pustules on leaves. These are commonly called *rusts* but this is a misleading name as scientists restrict the term rust to the leaf spots caused by a very special group of fungi. Black spot on roses or anthracnose on beans are typical leaf spots.

There are many other types of plant disease symptoms seen on the aerial parts of plants, but the diseases which seem to annoy gardeners most are the troubles which afflict the roots. Many of these are simply called *wilts* or *root rots* and the damage is usually first noticed when the plant wilts at midday in the summer. In the early stages of such wilts the plants may recover during a wet period or even during the night, but in the end these plants if pulled out of the ground will be seen to have a miserable brown root system with very short roots, in many cases with a discoloration at the base of the stem which may be shrivelled and obviously weakened.

A very common type of wilt is known as 'damping-off' and this is primarily a wilt of seedlings which can totally destroy boxes of seedlings once it gains hold. Unlike many plant diseases it is very *non-specific*. This means that while black-spot on roses will only attack roses or gooseberry mildew will only go to gooseberries, the damping-off fungi will attack almost any type of seedling so it is a very dangerous disease indeed. Another non-specific disease is generally called Botrytis and it produces a black rot covered with a grey mould from which things like tiny grey pin-heads arise. This disease is very widespread in any conditions which are fairly close or damp so that it will attack cuttings as they are rooted or tomatoes if there is inadequate ventilation.

Root rots and wilts are very widespread and difficult to do much about. It is usually too late when you see the symptoms and since the fungi are in the soil it is almost impossible to kill them without sterilising great volumes of soil.

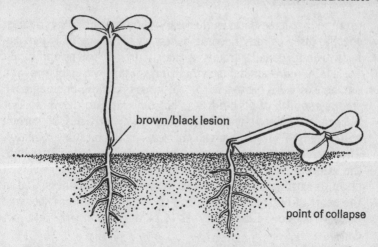

Figure 19 Seedlings damping-off. Note that the effect is at ground level where there is a film of moisture.

There are many other diseases, for example clubroot and peach leaf curl, and it is only good sense to have any affliction of your garden plants identified by an expert for the correct control methods may depend on an accurate identification. Notice the use of the word 'control' which is deliberate. Human beings can be cured of diseases, and insect pests can be killed and so further damage prevented, but there are no general methods that can be used to cure plants infected with a fungus or virus. At best we can hope to prevent the disease spreading to other plants and we can in many cases try to limit the spread within a single plant, if it is economically worthwhile, but we cannot induce the plant to replace the tissues damaged by fungal attack.

This thought leads directly to the idea which was advanced in the section about pests, but is even more important here, namely that prevention is better than cure. If this is reinforced with the knowledge that there is no cure, then prevention becomes the real basic aim. Of course we can't treat every plant all season to prevent every disease attacking but a spray of a good general fungicide such as Benonmyl applied early in the season will often reduce losses later in the year, when specific sprays against specific diseases may become necessary. This advice is particularly true for small gardens in the suburbs of towns and cities. For a hundred years industry in Britain was powered by coal and our houses were heated with coal fires. From the burning coal, smoke and filth of all kinds was belched out into the air so that it became polluted with gases and small particles of carbon which led to bronchitis and all sorts of respiratory diseases. Then came the Clean Air Acts and it became a crime to pollute the atmosphere. The effect was dramatic, for buildings stayed clean, breathing city air was no longer a risky business, and in the heart of busy industrial cities such as Manchester it became possible to grow different types of plants in the parks and gardens.

But no blessing is unmixed and gardeners began to notice an increase in the amount of black spot on roses, potato blight and many other plant diseases. This was due to the reduction in pollution. In the past the air had contained fine particles, mainly of sulphur, which fell on the plant leaves and coated them with a thin film of sulphur. This film acted as a chemical fungus killer, a *fungicide*, and so any spores of fungi which landed on such leaves were immediately killed and no disease developed. An early spray with a general fungicide which usually contains sulphur gives you all the advantages of a polluted atmosphere with none of the disadvantages.

One further aspect of many fungal and bacterial diseases is worth careful notice, and that is the so-called wound parasites. There are fungi (and Dutch elm disease is produced by such a fungus) which find it very difficult and in many cases impossible to attack whole, healthy plants, but if the plant is weakened in any way, can gain entry and set up serious disease. There are two obvious ways in which plants can be wounded and the best known is by pruning. Fruit trees, roses, and many shrubs and trees frequently require to be kept in shape or their size reduced, and doing this demands the removal of branches, so leaving an open wound. An open wound can be looked on as an open invitation to wood-rotting fungi to enter and attack and destroy the tissues which have been exposed. The fungus will then continue to grow into the tree killing and rotting as it goes so that in the end the whole tree is rotten and either falls in a strong wind or simply dies. To prevent this it is very sensible to coat exposed surfaces left after pruning with a layer of ordinary paint or with the special wound-sealing paints which speed up the healing of the wound (see Chapter 4).

The second important type of wound is that caused by insects, for as they suck their food from the tree or bore into the bark to lay their eggs they naturally leave a wound. Dutch elm disease gains entry to the host tree via the entry hole left in the bark by a beetle which not only makes the hole but also carries the spores of the disease with it. Greenfly (aphids) are the most important insects which spread disease for, as they move from plant to plant sucking food from the leaves, they tend to inject the leaves with any virus disease they may carry. For this reason stocks of nursery or seed crops which are virus-free are grown in remote areas where there are no adjacent infected crops from which the virus could be spread, and where the climate is not suitable for the build up and spread of greenfly.

Virus diseases are very widespread but are not easily recognised for the virus itself is very small and simple in structure so that it is forced to rely on the host plant to supply all its food. The virus therefore lives in very close and intimate contact with the cells of the host, being actually inside them but rarely doing enough damage to kill the host for that would be a form of biological suicide. All that happens therefore is that the host plant is weakened and becomes unthrifty. Often it will bear very poor and shrivelled fruit or only small potatoes which are scarcely worth digging. If the virus attacks a flower crop the petals may be distorted and ugly and when it attacks the leaves one finds that yellow areas develop, sometimes along the veins, sometimes all over the leaf, but always to the detriment of the plant.

Those mottled leaf symptoms are called *leaf mosaics* and are the usual sign that all is not well. Since there is no cure for plant virus diseases the only thing which can be done is to pull up and burn infected plants and so prevent further spread of the disease. Spraying with a good *aphicidal* solution will help to reduce the greenfly population and so reduce or eliminate the chance of the virus disease spreading quickly and widely.

Pest and disease control

When the beginner thinks of pest and disease control he conjures up visions of shelves laden with cans full of strange chemicals with even stranger names which will be a sure way to healthy, good cropping plants. This is a mistake. The real control of pests and disease starts very much earlier than this. Plants growing in a good rich soil with ample water and food supplies must always be the aim and to achieve this you have to start with the type of plant grown. If your garden is full of clubroot, then there is not much point in trying to grow cauliflowers, or if all your neighbours get canker in their parsnips then you must look for resistant or immune varieties of parsnips such as Avonresister. If your allotment is infested with potato root eel-worm then grow varieties such as Maris Piper or Pentland Javelin which have some resistance to this disease. In other words, you must start off by finding out which diseases are prevalent in your district and then use varieties of plant which are immune or have some resistance to these diseases. Remember the old saying about 'horses for courses' and you will at least start off right.

Next you must think about the soil in which you are growing the plants, and ask yourself what you grew there last year. A sensible gardener will then plant a different crop so that any pests or diseases left over from last year will not find the same easy food supply this year. This is one of the reasons for *crop rotation* which you will find discussed in full in *Growing Vegetables* in this series.

Another point about the soil is the amount of moisture it contains and, what is equally important, the humidity of the air above it. Fungi like damp conditions. This is specially true of fungi living in the soil for not only will they grow more rapidly in a moist soil but since a large number of fungal spores actually swim, the disease will spread more easily and further if there is a film of water over the soil. The term damping-off of seedlings accurately describes the conditions under which the disease occurs and spreads. The solution therefore is to ensure that soil drainage is good.

The importance of atmospheric humidity can scarcely be over-estimated and many will wonder how the ordinary gardener can affect, and to a certain extent control, such a factor. The answer lies in the magic words *air drainage* which really means the ease and therefore the speed with which moist or saturated air can be removed or drained away. Here it is important to introduce the term *microclimate*. This is a concept which is proving to be of great importance in gardening. It simply puts a name, and therefore directs attention, to the fact that very small local areas have a climate which can be very different from that of the big world around them. In gardening the most obvious example is a greenhouse or a cloche but to get the idea down to the right level, imagine a box of seedlings. The air around the box may be quite dry but the air between and among the seedlings will be more or less static. This means that if the box is overwatered, this static air will become saturated and unless this air is moved and displaced by drier air then the seedlings will be growing in a continuous film of water, hence encouraging damping-off.

What is needed therefore is air drainage. To be sure that there is adequate movement of air between and among the seedlings, they should not be sown too thickly or pricked out in rows in seed boxes, pans or pots so close together that there can be no air movement between the seedlings.

On a larger scale, a number of lawns may be very mossy simply because the grass is cut so infrequently that it gets long enough to ensure a very humid microclimate near the ground and this moisture encourages moss at the expense of grass.

To the practical gardener therefore the best advice is not to try to cram a quart into a pint pot and always to leave enough space between your plants to allow good air drainage. This will pay dividends in reducing the amount of damage done by diseases and insect pests.

But no matter what the gardener does in the way of better growing conditions, more careful choice of varieties or crop rotation, in the end some of his crops are bound to suffer attack from some source or other. The usual sources are the next-door gardens or the fields near or around the home, and if you try to shut out such wind-blown infection by growing a tall hedge then the problem becomes more complex because not only are hedges hiding places for trouble in the winter, but hedges create their own microclimate of still air, maybe shade, and even at a distance from the hedge, of some air turbulence on windy days. Most gardeners have to resort to other methods of pest and disease control and these fall into two very convenient categories, namely *biological* and *chemical*.

Biological pest and disease control

Biological control is based on the idea of using another organism to kill the particular pest or fungus disease, or to ward off the attack. Clearly this would be an ideal method for there would be no nasty chemicals involved, it would seem at first sight to be cheap and it would be very selective.

If we take a simple example, the pros and cons of such techniques become obvious, so let's consider greenfly and ladybirds. It has been known for years that ladybirds feed on greenfly, so that if the grower could introduce ladybirds to his aphid-infested roses, the ladybirds would eat the aphids, leaving the rosebud pest-free and then would either die themselves (from lack of aphids) or else start eating other insects. Put like that it sounds marvellous and undoubtedly has great popular appeal, but there are a number of snags in the method. For example, how do we get the ladybirds in the first place? The answer could be to raise them artificially, but to do that we may have to feed them on greenfly and so we move into the aphid growing business too, and that becomes costly as well as being a bit silly from a logical point of view. Another difficulty in biological control is that much-vaunted 'balance of nature', which simply means that numbers of different organisms are held in a rough equilibrium. Therefore if ladybirds are plentiful they will eat lots of greenfly. As the numbers of greenfly fall so also must the numbers of ladybirds (there will be a food shortage) and if the greenfly get too scarce the ladybirds die of starvation. But any greenfly left have now a ladybird-free environment and so they will multiply unchecked thus needing a fresh introduction of ladybirds.

The seesaws will therefore go on and the balance could swing to and fro benefiting the gardener sometimes and the greenfly at others. It may be argued that the ladybirds may eat *all* the greenfly and then just die out leaving the garden free of both greenfly and ladybirds. This of course would be a very drastic alteration in the balance of nature which should be avoided, but it would also be rather pointless for greenfly would come from other gardens, repopulate the rose beds and you are back where you started. Why should it be greenfly which come back to the garden rather than ladybirds? Well, there are many more greenfly than ladybirds so that the chances are greater, and if a ladybird came into the garden it would die, but if a greenfly came in it could multiply until some ladybirds got established and caught up with it. The seesaw again!

Having stressed the difficulty, it must at once be pointed out that biological control has had some spectacular successes and especially in a closed situation, such as a greenhouse or on an island, biological control may be very effective. For example there is a small wasp which will devour whitefly and these wasps can be bought each year and when introduced into an infested greenhouse will rid it of whitefly very quickly. But notice that in a greenhouse the chance of reinfection is much reduced. Biological control has proved both effective and economically viable in many situations and could be regarded as the ideal solution to many problems, but although research goes on apace, it is still only a very small number of pests and diseases which can be treated in this fashion. Gardeners are forced to look towards chemical fungicides and pesticides to achieve control of most disease or pest situations.

Chemical pest and disease control

The use of chemicals to kill insect pests and fungi is of great antiquity; for example, the Romans used pitch containing sulphur as a fuel for producing smoke which was allowed to drift through the olive groves and vineyards. In the Bible one of the seven plagues of Egypt was of locusts (insects) and all sorts of strange—and in some cases—useful substances were used for disease and pest control. With the application of science more efficient chemicals were developed until now there is an absolute plethora of products to be seen in any garden shop.

It would be pointless here to go into the details of what to use, where and when, but it is of great importance that certain principles are understood and followed to get the maximum benefit and the minimum disadvantage from the chemicals available.

In the beginning the trouble must be correctly diagnosed, for it is of no value at all to apply a chemical which controls greenfly when the problem is caterpillars, and plant diseases are much more difficult for the amateur to identify. Another point has already been made but it justifies repetition, namely control measures should be taken as early as possible *before* serious damage is done.

Too many gardeners think chemicals have almost magical powers but this is not so, and another of the golden rules is to be sure to follow up the initial treatment with a second and maybe a third after the appropriate interval. These later treatments should eliminate any pests or diseases you missed in the first spray as well as coping with later reinfections.

Because so many errors and losses of crops are caused by carelessness, the directions on the packages should be followed very carefully. If you apply the chemical in too great a concentration you may harm the plant and if the spray is too weak you may not kill the pest or disease, so if you use chemical sprays be sure you get the strength right.

Basically there are two types of chemical for control purposes : those which put a surface coating on the plant and those which penetrate the plant and are not *on* it but are *in* it. The latter have been developed fairly recently and are classed as *systemic* fungicides and insecticides. They are very effective because they are distributed by the plant itself to all its parts so that there are no unprotected places. As the plant grows so the systemic substances are moved into the new leaves etc., so maintaining a complete cover.

One of the difficulties with systemic insecticides is that many are harmful to man and to use them on food crops could be unwise. Packages of such substances very clearly instruct that they must not be used within a given period before collecting and eating the crop and these instructions must be rigidly followed. Similarly there are systemic fungicides which give the same protective properties, but are not so widely used as they might be.

In order to understand the problem faced by the chemist, it is as well to state the contradictory demands with which he is often faced. If he produces systemic substances then many are poisonous, but they will be much more effective protectants than simple sprays, which are washed off by rain and which cannot protect new growth.

He may be asked then to produce chemicals with a short life in the plant so that crops will not be made poisonous, but if he does that then the crop will require many frequent sprayings for complete protection.

He is also faced with the difficult choice between the broad and the narrow spectrum substances. In its simplest terms a broad-spectrum insecticide will kill all or nearly all insects, and the broad-spectrum fungicides, all fungi. This looks a good thing at first glance for it does away with the need to keep a whole range of substances in the garden shed. One will do. It also means that there is no worry about which insect pest is eating your plants because one insecticide will kill them all, and so it eliminates the need for accurate identification. However because it is non-selective the insecticide will kill everything, including what are called the 'friendly insects' such as ladybirds, lace wings, and ground beetles which play such a big part in keeping down the populations of many plant pests. For example ground beetles eat the larvae of cabbage root fly which can cause very serious damage in gardens.

A narrow spectrum substance will ideally only kill the pest or disease at which it is aimed. It demands a high standard of identification for unless the pest or disease is correctly diagnosed much money and effort can be misspent. For example, greenfly are not affected by many insecticides and severe infestations will positively thrive on a nicotine spray which kills other insects. For greenfly a spray based on malathion or dimethoate would be required.

Finally chemicals will obviously affect the environment and this may be for the worse as in the case of DDT whose use is now limited in many countries because it tends to accumulate in certain animals and birds. But all control has to be seen in a social context, for many countries once riddled with malaria are now free of this deadly disease thanks to the use of DDT to kill the carrier mosquito, and people there would not seek to ban such a valuable chemical. It must, however, be kept constantly in mind that although man must fight nature a lot of the time, it may be wiser in the very long term to work with her as far as possible without starving the human race.

So the problem is clear although the answer is not, and for the time being the grower is obliged to take the best advice he can get and then think over the implications before he applies it.

Common problems and queries

1. *Many insecticides and fungicides are poisonous to man. Is there any chance of them being taken in by the plant which if eaten by us will be poisonous also?*

This is one of the most important points that the pest chemist has to bear in mind. There are two groups of chemicals used in disease control which are very poisonous to man. The first is the heavy metals and of these mercury is by far the most common, for it is part of calomel dust used to control clubroot and cabbage root fly, while copper is very widely used in Bordeaux Mixture and a number of other fungicidal sprays. There has been little if any evidence of these metals getting into plants in any quantity and gardeners can feel perfectly safe in using them.

The other group of chemicals has already been mentioned, namely the insecticides based on organic phosphorus compounds. Most of these are very poisonous and do penetrate into the tissues acting as systemic compounds. Fortunately they have a limited life in the plants, but it can be as long as two weeks before they are rendered harmless, so that maximum care should be taken if they are used. The most poisonous chemicals such as parathion are no longer available to amateurs.

In order to keep things in perspective it must be remembered that poisonous chemicals have been used for centuries to kill insects and in fact many of the sticky fly papers which used to hang in houses before the Second World War were impregnated with compounds of arsenic, and calomel and corrosive sublimate were widely used. Nicotine which is still widely used is a very poisonous substance, and the problem arises not because such poisons are new but because we are much more alive to the dangers which they can pose than we used to be.

2.*What are puffer packs?*
When a finely ground fungicidal or insecticidal powder is enclosed in a soft plastic container with a nozzle, it is very easy to squeeze it sharply and release a small cloud of the dust. Such packs are of very little use outside, but can be of great use in the still, moist air of a greenhouse. There they can be used against green and whitefly, or the powder may be dissolved in a carrier substance which is a liquid and the pack then is an aerosol. These are quite effective but remember that the aerosol should only be used at a distance of about 10 cm (4 in) from the leaf surface otherwise the droplets are not given the space to spread and some damage can be done to the leaf by the concentrated spray.

The main use for the dry powder is as a seed disinfectant, especially on early-sown seed. If seed is sown when the ground is cold and wet there is a real chance that it will absorb water and swell but the temperature be too low for germination changes to proceed. In this semi-germinated state the seed can easily be attacked by fungi and go mouldy in the soil. Such seeds usually die or produce weak and often misshapen seedlings.

Before seed is sown therefore, if a few puffs of a good seed dressing are blown into the packet and it is then closed and shaken, there is every chance that each seed will have a fine coating of the fungicidal dust. Not only will this fungicide protect the seed from fungal attack, it will also help to sterilise a small area of soil around the seed and when the new root emerges it will at the very outset be growing in a friendly and not a hostile environment.

Such precautions are not necessary for late-sown seed, but are always advisable for early-sown seed. It is now possible to buy dressed seed of some flowers and vegetables.

3. *What can I do about slugs which cause more damage to my garden than insects or fungi?*

Sad to say effective slug control is one of the great unsolved problems of the amateur gardener. This is not to say that nothing will kill them for there are lots of slug killers on the market based on a chemical called methiocarb, or metaldehyde. The problem is complicated by the fact that slugs live in the soil and feed on organic matter. This means that unless compost is well rotted it can act as a feeding ground for slugs and many organic gardeners have problems with this pest. Because slugs move about in the soil, being near the surface and active on wet cool days or at night, one is obliged to lay baits to trap them and for this reason slug killers are usually sold as little pellets which can be scattered in the threatened or affected area. Since the pellets are harmful to children and dogs, they should be covered with a slate or tile.

The problem would be much reduced in severity if the places where the slugs lay their eggs were treated in the winter. Likely places are under stones lining paths, along wooden edges, under long damp weed and grass vegetation around the edges of plots. Although it seems very simple, a good start to control would be the cutting short of the verges and hedge-bottoms in the autumn and winter of each year.

There is a fairly effective liquid slug killer but quite large doses must be applied before the chemical is able to penetrate to the deeper layers of the soil.

4. *Is there anything effective that can be done to protect friendly insects?*

Obviously specific narrow-spectrum insecticides which would only kill the pests is one answer, but there are so few of these that one is forced to adopt other measures. There is, for example, the use of systemic insecticides which since they circulate inside the plants would only kill those insects which either eat or suck the fluid out of leaves, and this does not include the friendly insects. It can be argued that if we kill the pests we are depriving the helpful insects of their food supply and so they in their turn might die. The whole argument therefore gets back to questioning the use of any form of insecticide and in our modern system that is essential. As I write there are reports of vast locust swarms building up in the Sudan and Ethiopia which if they move could eat up much of the vegetation of East Africa and cause misery and death by starvation unless they are killed somehow.

Much research work is going on to try to discover the most effective ways of combining chemical and biological control of insect pests. A clear case of such a scheme might be to use insecticides when only the pests were active, for example, to avoid killing bees in a garden or orchard by restricting spraying to periods when the flowers were not open. This technique is now used widely in apple orchards where a long series of sprays against codlin moth, apple scab and other pests is given, none of them during blossom time.

The whole ecological argument against chemical control is very complex as it involves not only biology but also economics, sociology, ethics and the ultimate in argument, the future of mankind himself, so it is wise to think very carefully before taking an extreme position or even before making judgements at all. The problem is discussed a little more fully in Chapter 8.

7

Protected Cultivation

Introduction

The term *protected cultivation* has a very wide application ranging as it does from large elaborate greenhouse structures, via cold frames and cloches to sun rooms, houses and porches. The term has even been used to include growing anything in any kind of soil in any kind of shelter. The need for such cultivation springs from the fact that in Britain we have quite a marked seasonal climate with cold wet winters and (hopefully) hotter dry summers, but in other countries the protection may be designed to protect the plants against the heat and drought of the hot season rather than in our case to protect them from frost and cold.

Another reason for protected cultivation is because a large number of our food and decorative plants are not native to Britain. For example, because grapes, tomatoes, and poinsettias all come from much warmer or drier climates than we can normally provide, we would be unable to grow them at all well unless they could be protected at some stages in their growth.

A still further reason for protected cultivation lies in the relative shortness of the period during which we are absolutely free of frosts. Thus in many parts of the country, seedlings or cuttings must be raised in an improved environment if they are going to be able to mature and ripen a crop before the autumn frosts cut them down. Protection, especially in the early stages of growth, allows us to lengthen the frost-free season artificially, or the use of a heated greenhouse makes plant growth almost independent of the season.

There is a final more modern reason for protected cultivation namely that it allows full control of all growth factors.

In reality, if energy were sufficiently cheap, the ideal growing house would be made with solid well-insulated walls and the temperature, light, feeding and watering regimes would make the plants inside such a growth chamber absolutely independent of external variations in weather. It would be an area in which literally any crop could be grown at any time of year when the market afforded the maximum profit. The snag to such ideal conditions is the very high cost of energy and of the monitoring equipment which would be necessary to check the various factors at all times of day or night and to switch heat, light and water on and off as the occasion demanded.

Even the simplest protective shelter can, however, be very significant to plant growth and to set out the general principles which underlie all shelters, it is simplest to start off by considering an ordinary unheated greenhouse.

Protected cultivation and temperature

It seems at first sight a bit obvious to ask what is the reason for the glass, for the simple answer is to let the light in and plants need light before they can grow well. There are other light-transparent materials with some advantages over glass; for example increasing use is being made of plastic sheeting in many forms, but although this plastic material is much cheaper than glass, the fact remains that it too is transparent. If we used a material through which light would not pass we would be obliged to light the growing house artificially. This costs money whereas daylight and sunshine are free, so a transparent shelter is cheaper to maintain.

But the light that comes into a greenhouse or any window for that matter does more than light the room, it also heats it. This phenomenon is often called the *greenhouse effect* and depends on the fact that heat and light are interconvertible. Consider a light bulb and how hot it gets. A cold light is much more efficient, for all the energy in it appears as light whereas in ordinary light bulbs only part of the electricity is used to produce light and the rest produces heat.

Without going into great detail, light and heat are both forms of energy which travel in waves, but the wavelength of light is shorter than that of heat. When sunshine comes into a greenhouse it hits the floor, the plants, the bench, in fact all surfaces exposed to it. Some of it is absorbed by these surfaces, some is reflected as light (as we see it) and some is reflected as heat. The wavelength of light is short enough for the reflected light to pass back out through the glass, but heat has too long a wavelength to pass through glass easily and so it accumulates in the greenhouse and heats it up. Everyone with a greenhouse knows that even on a sunny day in winter, it can be very cold outside but in the greenhouse it will be quite warm, although as soon as the darkness falls the temperature in the greenhouse will plummet.

For the same reasons, a sunny day in summer can produce very high greenhouse temperatures, so much so that all the doors and ventilators need to be opened and water sprayed on the floor to try to bring the temperature down and stop the heat damaging the plants.

There is at the same time a disadvantage in the heat properties of glass for, although heat waves do not pass through it easily, heat can be very quickly lost from the greenhouse because of the large glass surface which is being continually cooled at night by the air outside. In the day this cooling effect would not be noticed because it is outweighed by the greenhouse effect, but at night and in the winter it *is* noticed so that some form of heating is often necessary to come on at nightfall and stop the temperature falling too far. The obvious method to avoid heat loss through the glass is to double glaze but this is very expensive. However a home-made double glazing system can easily be made by lining the inside of the glass with transparent plastic film and so forming an air lock between the plastic and the glass through which the heat will pass to the outside very slowly indeed. This means that much of the heat accumulated through the day will protect plants from freezing temperatures at night.

The heat of a protected environment can be utilised by the amateur gardener in another way, namely to heat the soil. This is done in the open garden by using long tunnel cloches over the bare earth in an area where some seed will be sown. The plastic or glass cloches allow the light to get through and so the air in the cloches and the soil are heated by the greenouse effect. Normally this is not very important but in the case of early crops and early sown seed it could be vital.

The most difficult time for any plant is the seedling stage and this is almost entirely the consequence of inadequate root growth. Seeds sown in cold soil may take a long time to germinate and despite the use of seed dressings may be attacked and killed by soil fungi and bacteria. Even if the seed germinates safely, until an adequate root system is developed the seedling will be poorly supplied with food and water. The speed of development of the roots is much affected by soil temperatures. Thus in a cold soil roots develop very slowly, but in a warmer soil growth is quite rapid.

Therein lies the value of the cloche, for if put on the soil say two weeks before planting, it will cause the soil to warm up. When the seed is sown it will germinate quickly, roots will develop more quickly and the seedlings will be established and growing well that much sooner.

Protected cultivation and humidity

There is another very obvious benefit of protected cultivation which is often overlooked and that is the great reduction in exposure to the wind. This protection ensures that leaves won't be torn and that wind-borne pests and diseases will not obtain as easy access to the plants. There will also be a great reduction in water loss from the soil and from the leaves, for as every housewife knows, washing hung out in the garden will dry much more quickly on a windy day than on a still day. But this very advantage lays a trap for the unwary. Because water loss by the plant is so much reduced under protected cultivation, there is a great danger that such plants may be over-watered.

Consider a houseplant. It is not exposed to wind and is living in a good environment. Granted it will lose some water to the air, but the more it loses to the air of the room, the more humid the room becomes since the air it contains is not being replaced by fresh air in the wind. The rate of water loss will slow down and although it never (or rarely) stops, it can become a mere fraction of the loss from a similar plant outside. But people tend to be kind to plants and often work on the principle that regular watering is what plants need. This may be true, but the intervals between successive waterings should be much longer in winter when the temperature is low. Thus plants which require watering every other day in high summer, may only need water once a week in autumn or spring and only once a month in winter. More house-plants die of over-watering than any other cause, and although it is very difficult to judge the exact timing of watering, a fairly good rough and ready rule is that you should not water if the surface of the soil in the pot is damp, or only water when the soil surface is dry and remember plants suffer more from over- than from under-watering.

Because air in cloches and greenhouses tends to be static, it can become very humid. Such moist air is ideal for the build up of pests and diseases for there are none of the checks and balances of the outside within the cosy greenhouse. It therefore becomes absolutely essential to try to maintain as high a standard of hygiene as possible in such situations. Many growers change the soil regularly or in some cases will go to great lengths to sterilise it either by heat or by the use of chemicals such as dazomet. Another way of tackling the same problem is to grow the plants in sterile compost in pots, or in gro-bags, or even in bottomless rings. These bottomless rings are put on sand on a bench or on any medium, even soil, and are filled with good sterile compost in which the plants are grown. This not only ensures sterility, at least in the early stages, but also enables the grower to feed the plant by adding fertilisers directly into the ring.

For the grower with a little lean-to or a small greenhouse, the best method is to try to avoid these difficulties, and there are a series of steps that he should always follow to ensure that the greenhouse is at least clean at the beginning of the season.

1. Thoroughly wash down the greenhouse with a simple disinfectant each winter. Pay particular attention to the undersurfaces of staging, to the corners, and to the area around the water tank if there is one. Fumigate if necessary.

2. If you buy-in plants be very careful that you are not introducing pests or diseases into the greenhouse. If in doubt, then reject the plant.

3. Use sterile composts for potting and growing. There is a great temptation just to use soil from the garden and often you will get away with it, but resist the temptation and buy good materials in which to grow the crops.

4. Avoid over-stocking and crowding plants too close together. Crowded plants reduce air movement, provide lots of nooks and crannies in which pests and diseases can lurk, and if one plant gets infected then the disease will spread through the house like wildfire.

5. Remember that the most important part of any sheltered area is the ventilator. Good ventilation will produce stronger and healthier plants. Old gardeners talk about the air being 'buoyant' and this means fresh and not too moist.

6. Always remove yellowing leaves from the plants and from the house because they will act as centres from which deadly diseases such as Botrytis Grey Mould can spread to practically any plant in the greenhouse, especially if the humidity is high.

7. Never water the greenhouse last thing at night for as the temperature falls so the humidity rises, and if the air becomes cool enough there may be a film of dew formed on the leaves and this encourages the spread of disease. Always water first thing in the morning and only damp down at night if necessary.

Protected cultivation and light

It is almost inevitable that as one tries to protect plants against extremes of temperature there is always the possibility that light will be reduced by the means of protection. This, of course, is the reason why plant shelters are made of glass or transparent plastic, for without light, or even in reduced light, plants do not grow very well.

The question then arises of how efficient such structures are at allowing light to pass into them. The short answer to this question is that they are very efficient indeed, and this is especially true when the cloche, greenhouse, or cold frame is first built. But as time passes this efficiency decreases until in an old structure the light intensity can be very much reduced..

The main cause of this reduction in light is simply dirt which, when it is allowed to settle on glass or plastic, begins to encrust it. In some areas where heavy industry predominates this dirt has the ability almost to etch the glass so that the particles of dirt, usually carbon, get lodged in these fine cracks in the surface and are almost impossible to remove. For this reason alone any glass structure should be thoroughly washed down both inside and outside at least once each year. It is most important that this washing is done as early in the autumn as possible, for the shortage of light becomes most acute in the winter when we have so many dull grey days, and every effort should be made to take full advantage of such light as there is. Coverings made of plastic are even more likely to suffer from scratches on the surface, unless they have been specially treated, but since plastic is relatively cheap and easy to remove and replace, it is much more satisfactory to have a completely fresh plastic skin every third year if you think light is being kept out.

When the light decreases in intensity and because of the shorter days in the winter, it is wise to get the plants you are overwintering as near to the glass as possible. This is usually done by having removable shelves which can be slung on brackets or wires fixed to the wooden spars of the roof of the greenhouse. In late winter and early spring as soon as any seedlings are through they should be moved to a similar position so that they will grow short and sturdy. A spindly drawn seedling is much more likely to succumb to damping-off than one which is short, dark green and strong.

Many houses have lean-to greenhouses where the wall of the dwelling forms the back long wall of the greenhouse. When this is the case the wall should be painted white if at all possible so that it will reflect and not absorb light. This will make a very great difference to the light in the greenhouse as also will painting the staging, the door and general woodwork white to aid light reflection.

When washing a greenhouse particular care should be taken to clean the areas of glass overlap for it is in these small areas, where the two sheets of glass create their own microclimate, that the green slimy algae can grow and these are very efficient shutters-out of useful light. These thin overlapping strips may seem of little significance, but if the total area they occupy in the roof of the greenhouse or a cold frame is calculated it becomes quite significant. This disadvantage is avoided by the use of clear plastic film in which there are no overlaps.

The same problem also arises when a greenhouse is being bought, and the pros and cons are discussed in the volume on greenhouses in this series, but briefly one can say that wooden greenhouses tend to have broader roof beams than metal (usually aluminium) greenhouses, so that they reduce the light more. On the other hand since wood does not conduct heat from inside the greenhouse to outside, the rate of heat loss from a wooden structure is very much less than that from aluminium, which is a good conductor. There are therefore arguments on both sides, but most of the modern commercial growers seem to be coming down in favour of metal houses whereas most domestic growers prefer the more attractive aesthetic appeal of wood. The reason for the commercial choice lies in the fact that it is usually rather cheaper to heat the greenhouse that little bit more than it is to provide additional light maybe all day every day in the winter.

Protected cultivation and biological factors

In this section of the chapter it is merely a matter of underlining points already made, and extrapolating ideas already advanced to their logical conclusion. Greenhouses and other protected environments are designed to protect plants against the vicissitudes of the climate outside, but by the very same logic, the pests and diseases of the plants are equally or even more protected. The additional protection springs from the fact that, in a clean greenhouse, there should be no pests or diseases and therefore none of the *friendly* insects or the spells of inclement weather which keep the pest population in some degree of control outside. If a single pest gains entry it then has all the plants in the greenhouse on which to feed so that multiplication is rapid and easy and an epidemic can build up very quickly. On the other hand, if an insect which eats plant pests gains entry to a clean greenhouse, it will immediately die because there are no pests on which it can feed. Of course, it is impossible to keep a stock of friendly insects in the greenhouse because to feed them one would need to introduce the pests one is trying to avoid.

The conclusion is that in almost any system of protected cultivation the harmful organisms are bound to be at a considerable advantage. This is the fundamental reason why cleanliness should be maintained at all costs and any yellowing or dying leaves which could harbour pests or diseases be removed at once.

On the other hand, because protected cultivation is applied to limited and usually enclosed areas, methods of pest and disease control which would be inappropriate outside become perfectly feasible in such an enclosed area. For example, it is possible to fumigate a greenhouse and kill red spider, weevils, Botrytis and so on whereas outside the fumigant would either be blown away or dispersed by the wind and the necessary concentration and penetration of chemical might never be obtained. Similarly biological control becomes much more feasible. The use of the little wasp *Encarsia formosa* which will eat all the whitefly in a greenhouse is a very rapid and cheap method of control which is much less effective in larger field areas.

One area of inside infection is undoubtedly the water tank, especially when rain water is collected from the roof of the greenhouse and then stored inside. Naturally, such water is soft and very pure but it will contain spores and pests which have been deposited on the glass panes of the roof. In and around the water tank these pests find a good warm and moist microclimate and they will therefore flourish. Accordingly all such tanks should be emptied, scrubbed clean and maybe washed out with a mild disinfectant once each year at least.

The other major hazard is the soil, and in it all sorts of troubles, such as root rots and wilts, may be stored up. This point has been considered in Chapter 6 on pests and diseases, but the best and easiest generalisation to make is that usually in the end it becomes cheaper and more satisfactory for the beginner to buy sterile composts and grow his crops in pots, gro-bags or rings.

Common problems and queries

1. *What is the best site for a greenhouse, and should it run north/south?*

Since we have so much cloudy overcast weather, greenhouses should never be sited in shade whether it comes from trees or buildings. In the winter, the lack of light produced by cloudy skies and shade will produce drawn, weak plants. The big argument in siting a greenhouse is whether it should run north/south or east/west, and the basis of the argument is that in Britain the sun is always to the south, especially in winter. If the greenhouse runs east/west the sunshine will hit the length of the house so that in winter particularly there will be the maximum light. Thus for a greenhouse dedicated to winter or early crops the east/west situation is advantageous.

However, the position is reversed in summer. In the north/south position the sun will shine between the rows of plants and in the summer all plants will receive an equal amount of all the available light, but in the east/west position, the first row of plants will shield the next row and so on with the final result of very unequal light distribution and so an uneven crop. So the immediate answer to the question is that it all depends on how you intend to use the house and for which crops. Winter crops benefit from an east/west and summer crops from a north/south greenhouse.

Lean-to houses should face south or west, for in the north or east location they would be in shade much of the time. To my mind much of the argument is academic for the amateur should be using his greenhouse all the year round so any good flat open situation will produce good results.

2. *I have heard that plastic sheets will keep out much of the light needed by plants. Is this true?*

It is certainly true that not all transparent materials will transmit the same kinds and quantities of light but there is no reason to doubt the efficiency of modern plastic sheeting in allowing perfectly normal plant growth. The universal use of polythene (or other plastic) tunnels and cloches in recent years would not have occurred had there been any doubts in the mind of commercial growers that the quantity and quality of the crops they were protecting was in any way inferior when compared with those grown under glass.

3. Why are many greenhouses shaded in the summer?

The reason for the shading, usually with a white emulsion, is to reduce the light getting into the greenhouse in the bright hot days of summer. Of course this reduces the intensity of the light but by so doing it also reduces the greenhouse effect. The net result is that the temperature may be as much as 20° lower in a shaded when compared with an unshaded house.

A number of our greenhouse crops and plants are not natives of tropical hot climates, and at high temperatures a number of things can happen, all of which may harm the plants. For example, the roots may not be able to take up water as quickly as the leaves are losing it and so the leaves will wilt and may develop scorch symptoms. The development of flowers or even the efficiency of pollination may be impeded and crops such as tomatoes may suffer in consequence. Lastly because of the high temperatures and the rapid removal of water from the soil, there will be a need for an increased frequency of watering and very often this is not possible if the owner is away all day at work. Again this can lead to wilting and even death.

There is one moral which must be drawn from all that has been said, namely that, in the summer, the danger to plants in a greenhouse lies rather in extreme heat than in cold, so that it is essential that *maximum* ventilation be maintained all day, and that adequate ventilation be obtained at night.

4. There are many mechanical gadgets available to control environments. Are they worthwhile?

Most of the so-called mechanical aids to greenhouse gardening act by means of sensors which, if the air temperature drops below a certain level, will automatically switch on some sort of heating system. Similar sensors will control the humidity or, if the temperature is too high, will open ventilators. In fact they will operate to control nearly every aspect of the controlled environment.

These are very excellent machines which certainly make life much easier for those who can afford them (an automatic waterer is an absolute boon) but they are by no means essential if the owner of the greenhouse is willing to take the trouble to open and close ventilators. To many growers the great virtue of such devices is that they eliminate the human factor of forget-fulness, although complete reliance on such systems is unwise because they do occasionally break down.

5. What are the particular virtues of soil-warming cable?
Many growers are so concerned with getting the air temper-ature right that they forget the roots which are very much con-trolled by soil temperature. Normally most plants will do very well if nature is allowed to take its course but there are a few occasions on which a little help does not go amiss.

Soil-warming cable should be laid in a snake-like fashion about 15 cm (6 in) below the soil surface. There are special types of cable for this purpose and the amateur must take advice from an electrician on this point, for remember that soil is wet and water conducts electricity, so the insulation should be perfect. It should be appreciated that even in a cold frame or greenhouse a certain amount of soil cultivation is necessary and care should be taken not to damage the cable with trowels, spades or any cultivating tool.

Such cable can be used to hasten the rooting of cuttings and the germination of seeds. Because the soil is heated it will tend to dry out more quickly and care should be taken to ensure that enough soil moisture is available to allow the plants to derive the full benefits from the soil heat.

Early crops can be grown very successfully in a heated frame and already many salad crops for winter use are raised on this principle. A succession of early crops could be lettuce under-sown with carrots and followed by cauliflowers. Growers have had success with chicory, endive, asparagus, melons, marrows, radishes and other vegetables grown out of season. Even strawberry plants can be forced into early fruiting and tomatoes will get away to an early start if their feet are warm. Read *Electricity in Horticulture* by A. E. Canham (Churchill, 1964).

8

The Importance of the Environment

Introduction

The modern use of the word *environment* tends to have emotive connotations and is usually used in connection with some aspect of conservation. In fact, however, the environment is an omnibus word used to denote the collection of factors—climatic, or relating to the soil, or chemical, or even biological—which make up the background against which all plants grow and develop. It is a useful word but it is also a misleading word as it tends to draw attention to the whole without mentioning the parts which make up that whole, and if the environment is to be studied fruitfully and used for the benefit of mankind, then that study has to be done piece by piece before the pieces can be put together and general conclusions perhaps drawn.

A further complication when considering the environment arises from the way in which each part affects many other parts. To take the simple example of temperature, if we raise the temperature we also affect the humidity, the rate of chemical reactions in the soil and maybe in the plant. We may raise it so high that water shortage becomes a problem and only specially adapted plants and animals can survive. In other words if we alter one aspect of the environment, then that alteration can set up a chain of events the end of which is very hard to foresee, and it would be a very foolish person who would make *ex cathedra* statements about the ultimate consequences of any change in an environmental factor. This makes experiments about the effects of changes in the environment on plants difficult to interpret.

However it must not be allowed to stifle research but rather serve as a warning about glib or facile conclusions. What this chapter will do is attempt to divide the environment into a number of constituent parts and show the ways in which each factor can affect a plant's growth. The environment will vary even in a small garden and the best use of the ground will be made if this variation is taken into account.

Physical factors

1. Temperature—frost

In Britain we are very rarely troubled by high temperatures but they do occur and the summers of 1975 and 1976 were very good examples of excessive heat. When this happens, the heat is also accompanied by a lack of water and so we have a drought. Thus the environmental effect is not that of temperature alone and so is difficult to interpret. High temperatures will be considered under the section on 'drought' when water supply has been examined.

The effects of frost are much better understood and it is possible to divide plants into those perennials, such as most trees and shrubs, which can withstand frost, and annuals which are usually killed at the first frost. Of course many trees and shrubs *are* frost tender and the only places in Britain where they can be grown are the Scilly and Channel Islands or the extreme West of England, Wales, Scotland and Ireland, where the presence of the sea stops any severe frosts.

When a frost-hardy plant is exposed to very low temperatures a number of chemical reactions take place which usually involve the change of starches into sugars. This means that in the cells of the plants, instead of a watery sap containing grains of starch, there will be a thick sugary syrupy liquid. Other changes take place as well and the outcome is that the cells of frost-hardy plants become filled with a kind of plant anti-freeze.

In plants which cannot perform this trick or do it too slowly the watery sap will begin to freeze and ice crystals will form. Since water expands as it freezes, the crystals take up more room than the water did and so some of the cells may be ruptured and will die. This is the same process which causes water pipes to burst when frozen.

Observant readers will have noticed the phrase 'or do it too slowly' in the last paragraph and this is of importance to gardeners, for you can literally train plants to perform this trick and so gain frost hardiness. The technique is called *hardening-off* and simply involves exposing the plants for increasingly longer periods of time to lower temperatures so that they gradually acclimatise themselves. It is impossible to be dogmatic about times of hardening off other than to say that it is safer to harden your plants off too slowly than to put them outside before they can stand the colder conditions. Nature itself will harden off most plants in the autumn and so the technique is best employed by the gardener in the spring.

Plants for an early crop will be reared in a cold frame where they are protected from frost. As they age and the time comes near for them to be put out in the garden, the lights of the frame are raised for an increasing period of time each day. This exposes the plants to outside conditions for longer and longer periods (during which they learn these biochemical tricks) until such time as they can be planted out. At that time of year (April/May) there is always the chance of a sudden snap frost but if the plants have been carefully hardened off, there is little need for fear.

Another important scientific point for gardeners is that cold air is heavy and will run downhill exactly as if it were water if there is warmer air at a lower level. The tenderest shrubs and plants should therefore never be put in a valley between two hills for all the cold air will drain down there. In exactly the same way as water can be dammed by a barrier so can cold air, and if your garden is in a natural hollow the skilful use of hedges and other barriers can guide the frosty air away from your most tender plants into a less easily damaged part of the garden. If you are forced to use the lowest area where cold air accumulates (often called a *frost pocket*) it sometimes pays to plant relatively tall subjects there, for their tops could well be above the layers of cold air. But clearly the ideal site would be one on a gentle slope where air drainage would be free.

2. Water—flood and drought

As was seen in Chapter 2, water in the soil plays many roles and is vital to the well-being of the plant. But it is possible to have too much of a good thing and a marshy wet garden, or one which floods regularly, can pose many difficult problems. Of course the obvious solution is to lime the soil to improve the drainage and to put in tile or sump drains, but this is not always possible, for drainage demands an outfall, a place where the water can go, and this may simply not exist. In such cases it is pointless to go to enormous expense to drain undrainable land. It is very much better to accept the situation and try to make the best of it. Raised beds can be made which will drain into the surrounds or be above the water level and in these beds a wide range of moisture-loving plants can be grown. Alternatively, an artificial lake or pool can act as a sump and be used to grow water lilies and other water-loving plants.

Gardeners can be reassured about periodic floods for they rarely do any permanent damage. Of course you won't get a beautiful lawn if it is flooded half the winter, but because plants are so tough you will be surprised how they will recover. The use of small trees such as willows, alder and hazel, will help to dry the soil by removing lots of water from it when the drier weather comes so that other plants can be grown. The point to remember is that flooded soil has fertiliser washed out very quickly, so growers will need to add food after the floods are over and may need to add it at a slightly higher rate than usual.

The normal condition in Britain is of a slight drought in the summer. Although it comes as a surprise to most people, there are very few areas of the country where the addition of irrigation water does not help the crop. But drought is only important when it is widespread and prolonged and the recent dry summers have made this point very fully.

When a plant is exposed to high temperatures normally the leaves are kept cool by the evaporation of water through the stomata, but if there is a shortage of water, then wilting occurs, the leaves may get scorched and, if this is prolonged, irreversible chemical changes take place and the plant dies. Obviously the effects of drought will be most severe in thin sandy soils which have little moisture-holding powers, and here is another obvious reason for the use of as much humus/compost as possible in the soil.

Since the real killer is prolonged drought, early crops which have a shorter growing season and which may have bulked their crop before the drought really takes hold, have a much better chance of succeeding than late crops. No gardener of course wants to fill his garden with early potatoes or early peas but such crops should never be discarded and some should always be grown as insurance.

Another significant point about early crops is that, if sowings or plantings of late crops begin to fail, they should be replaced by *early* varieties which will have a chance to produce yields before the frosts of autumn come.

Roots, of course, grow best where there is a good supply of water, and there is a very good evidence to show that they will actively grow towards water. This should always be borne in mind if you are forced to water a crop during a drought for it means that many light sprinklings of water will simply encourage surface roots to develop and these are in the most vulnerable place if the drought is prolonged. The conclusion therefore is that water should never be added to the soil in small quantities; it is much better to use the water to soak a limited area thoroughly than to spread it thinly over the whole garden.

As a corollary any watering should be done in the cool of the evening when it will get a chance to soak down into the soil and will not be immediately dried off by the heat of the sun.

So far as is possible the surface of the soil should be protected from the drying rays of the sun and this is best done by using a thick mulch. Of course if you put the mulch on dry soil and the mulch itself is dry, then any rain or moisture that is available would simply be soaked up by the mulch and the soil and so the plant roots would get very little if any at all. For this reason it is always best to apply a mulch early in the season, say in May when the soil is wet, for not only will it help to conserve the soil moisture but it will also act as a weed smother or, if the weeds are not killed, will make them much easier to uproot.

Remember too that it is unwise to water a soil covered by a

mulch, for the organic material will soak up much of the water. Rather the mulch should be carefully raked off, the water then applied directly to the soil and the mulch replaced. This will ensure that it will get down to the plant roots and do the maximum good.

Lawns suffer very badly in a drought especially if they are badly drained. Such a lawn has mainly surface roots and is therefore very susceptible to drought damage, not only from the direct effect of the weather on the grasses but also because weeds are very often deep-rooted and can tap water supplies which are deep. If you look at a lawn containing clover in a drought you will often find that the clover is dark green and thriving while the grass is yellow and dying. Two points follow. Firstly, it is patently absurd to cut lawns very short in dry periods: the grass should be left as long as is decently possible in order to protect the soil surface and conserve what water there may be. The second point is that, although normally one should remove the mowings from the lawn because they not only contain weed seeds but will also tend to build up an organic-rich surface layer which can hinder drainage, in a drought the lawn mowings act as a surface mulch and will help to reduce water loss if they are simply left where they fall.

Because of the reduced competition from the grass and their own good growth, weeds will spread during a drought and special care should be taken to kill the weeds and feed and encourage the grass to grow as soon as the weather breaks and more moisture is available. This means that you should apply fertiliser (preferably an autumn dressing) and follow about ten days later with a good selective weed-killer.

3. Light
Of all the factors which affect plants light has probably the greatest number of influences. In previous chapters photosynthesis and photoperiodicity were briefly discussed but there is still a great deal to be said about the formative effects of light. It is easiest to start off by reminding you of the appearance of plants grown in the dark; these could best be described as long and spindly and of a pale yellow colour with tiny almost scale-

like leaves. Such plants are said to be *etiolated*. We already know that light is essential for the formation of chlorophyll, so the yellow colour is easily explained. What is left to explain then is the spindly stem and the small leaves and it is because of these that light is said to have a *formative* effect.

If the spindly growths are examined closely, it can usually be shown that the stem has not grown more leaves than normal, but that there is a longer distance between the existing leaves when compared with a normally grown plant. In other words the internodes have elongated. As plants are exposed to more and more light the internodes shorten until in normal daylight plants are the normal height. Many botanists believe that many mountain plants are dwarf and almost like rosettes on the ground because the light can be very intense in high Alpine or Himalayan regions. (Of course, one must acknowledge that low temperatures and shortage of food may also play a critical part in the dwarfing.)

So far as the internal structure of the stem is concerned there is a clear lack of hard woody tissues in plants grown in the dark when compared with those which have developed in full light.

A similar response can be seen in plants grown in shade, be it from a hedge, the house, overhanging trees or adjacent buildings. The gardener's term to cover this is that the plants are *drawn*. Drawn plants are often seen in small gardens where the grower is trying to make a maximum use of the little space that is available, and one often sees an apple tree with long spindly potatoes being grown underneath it. In these conditions both types of plant suffer. The roots of the potatoes will compete for food with those of the apple tree and since potato roots are relatively shallow and so get the food first, the apple tree suffers. But the leaves of the apple get the light first, so the potatoes are in the shade, cannot photosynthesise efficiently and become drawn and weak.

In many cases the gardener will settle for less than the best from each crop, and on the 'horses for courses' basis will be quite happy, but it is certainly better, if there is a shade problem, to settle for *early* crops which will develop before the leaves of the shade tree or hedge are fully mature, or to prune and trim the shade-giver to allow maximum light. An alternative might be to grow crops such as radish or lettuce which are not light-demanding but of course there is only a limited number of suitable plants and these may not be the ones you want.

A further difficulty arises with drawn crops, for the stems are usually so weak that they sprawl and trail on the ground. There they tend to get intertwined and set up a microclimate which remains humid and is ideal for pests and diseases to become established.

So far we have not considered to what extent light affects flowers. Of course where a food crop is *not* being grown the question of yield might be thought to be unimportant, but it has been shown that in shade the actual number of flowers is reduced. What is probably much more important is that the brightness of the flower colour is much reduced and there is an increased tendency to greenfly and mildews. This colour effect even extends to leaves, and plants with coloured foliage such as *Rhus cotinus* and some pelargoniums are much more vivid and impressive when in full sun.

The herb garden is best in a fully sunny position because the essential oils which produce the flavour in thyme, bay and fennel are developed in quantity in good sunshine but seem to be reduced in effectiveness in plants grown in shade.

Lastly, there are no good rockeries or rock gardens which are heavily shaded. In such gardens one is trying to emulate mountainous conditions where there are no trees and the light is very intense, so that most rockery plants demand much sun and light, although some of them may prefer a fairly moist soil.

The best advice that can be given to the small garden owner is to plan your garden most carefully; if there is a shade problem use early plants such as bulbs and spring flowers in shady areas, choose well-recognised shade-lovers such as polyanthus, dicentra and astilbe and where the soil is suitable use evergreens which will be in leaf all the year round and so need to get light at all times. As far as possible try to avoid creating shade problems for yourself and for your neighbours.

The light problem in gardens is very much tied up with aspect and exposure. A garden facing north and east will be a cold, damp and late garden and owners of such gardens should recognise the fact and act accordingly. On a slope facing south-west the sun's rays will give the maximum benefit, and of course although such a garden will be more liable to drought, it will be ideal for early vegetable and flower crops and should avoid many lingering frosts.

Biotic factors

These are the effects on any given plant of all the other living things around it. Ideally, biotic factors must include insects and birds but since many of these have been discussed in the chapter on pests and diseases, it is proposed to concentrate in this section on the crop itself and on weeds and other plants.

1. *The crop itself*

Gardeners don't usually consider the effect of one cabbage on all the other cabbages in the row, but if you think about it for a moment you are bound to reach the conclusion that any plant will create the maximum competition for an identical plant. The reason for this is that identical plants are competing for the same food from the same depth of soil at exactly the same time, hence the acute competition. This is recognised by the spacing that is allowed between plants in the same row and in some cases even of the distance between the rows. Thus when you read a seed packet for summer cauliflower it could well advise planting them '60 cm (24 in) apart each way'. (See T. Biggs, *Growing Vegetables*, in this series.)

This distance has really been determined on the basis of trial and error and what is deemed the economically suitable size of cauliflower for the market. Until recently there has been very little research on this difficult problem of spacing, but since the establishment of the National Vegetable Research Station at Wellesborne, such difficulties are now being examined in detail. So far there is not a great deal to help the amateur grower of vegetables but there are many indications that the effects of competition are important and that this is a prime biotic factor.

The simplest way to explain this is to say that there seems to be a maximum yield that one gets from a given area of ground and if you crowd the plants close together you will get a large number of small plants such as onions or cauliflowers—but if you put a small number of plants in the same area, the same yield will show itself as fewer but larger onions or cauliflowers. This means that for a couple it is probably better to plant more closely and get a crop from each unit which is not too large and will be sufficient for a meal. If on the other hand there is a large family to feed each meal, then it would be wiser to space the plants more widely and so obtain fewer but larger units.

The best practical advice about growing vegetables is that you should consider the distances outlined in books and on seed packets as being possibly a maximum, and from that starting point reduce distances until the type of crop which is sought is obtained. Of course there will be disappointments but you will learn by trial and error.

2. Weeds

One of the greatest advances of modern crop science has been the development of selective and pre-emergence weed-killers. The reason for this is not difficult to appreciate for weeds are a very powerful competitive factor, taking away food, water and light from the crop and thus reducing yields. For centuries, therefore, gardeners have weeded their beds and plots with varying amounts of enthusiasm and diligence—not only were they reducing competition but the weeded plots also looked tidy and trim, although the finished article in no sense could be said to look natural.

Of the many pieces of advice which liberally besprinkle gardening, one of the most frequently used is 'you must keep the hoe moving'. The basis for this is that by continued hoeing weeds would be unable to become established and so the crop would not suffer. Hoeing, however, can be hard work and is only possible where individual crop plants are sufficiently widely spaced, both in and between drills, to allow room for the hoe to move. In fact one of the main factors which determined the distances between rows in the field was the amount of space needed for a horse, (or even a man on a tractor) to pull a hoe on a large area.

There are three aspects of weeding and of these the most quickly dismissed is the aesthetic appeal of a freshly weeded area, be it rose-bed or potato field. The plants and the flowers look better and greener set against the dark rich brown background of the soil, and to the enthusiast that in itself is sufficient to justify the practice and make the hard work worthwhile.

The second aspect of weeding is purely biological and concerns the way in which weeds can act as food for pests and diseases during the winter when there is no crop in the ground, or can provide shelter for slugs during hard frosts. This could be said to be an important reason for reducing the weed population, for effective garden hygiene begins with removal of affected crop plants and then proceeds to removal of weeds which harbour the pests and diseases.

But it is the way in which weeds are said to choke and strangle the crop which catches the attention and is the main reason for killing weeds either by chemicals or by using the hoe. A few statistics might make this clear. A paper published by Hewson, Roberts and Bard, in the 1973 *Journal of Horticultural Research*, provides good data on broad beans which show that, in a year in which there was a shortage of moisture, a reduction of 80% occurred in the bean yield when the crop was weedy. Of course, this is an extreme case, but even with fairly low, naturally occurring weed densities, decreases of 13 to 27% in yield resulted.

The significant thing however was their work on timing of weed eradication, for the crop can be kept weed free at different times and for periods of differing lengths. The results were surprising and could be very important both on a large (agricultural) or small (garden) scale, for they showed very clearly that 'if the crop was kept clean for the first one to one-and-a-half weeks, weeds that developed after this had no adverse effect on yield'. In further statements it seemed clear that if the weeds are removed no later than four weeks after 50% emergence of the crop, the final yield will be unaffected by the development of weeds subsequently.

These findings stress the great significance of competition in the early stages of crop growth, and the gardener should take very careful note and act on the belief that very good weed control is essential while the crop is still young, but thereafter, although the plot may look unsightly, there will be only a very small reduction in yield.

This makes the further point, which is very little appreciated by the small gardener, that the use of pre-emergence weed-killers could be one of his most valuable tools not only in improving yields but also in reducing work. Farmers have used these weed-killers for a number of years but until recently they have not appeared in a pack of a size suitable for amateurs. Now several such compounds are on the market and their sensible use can effectively reduce most of the weed competition in the early stages of growth.

Weed control around fruit bushes and shrubs is very important also and in the case of trees and shrubs with thick brown bark this can be easily achieved by the use of paraquat or diquat.

Chemical factors

If you mention 'environment' to any school child or even to most men in the street, they will expect you to talk about chemicals and pollution, but although the dangers are now widely recognised, it is folly to assume that all chemicals are bad or even dangerous. To try to look at the chemical factors in the environment impartially is almost impossible, but an attempt must be made.

The process of photosynthesis involves the use of CO_2 from the air and of H_2O from the soil and both these substances are chemicals. Of course they are common chemicals and we tend to think they are therefore harmless, but the folk who died in the Black Hole of Calcutta must have suffered from an excess of CO_2 so in fact although this chemical is harmless at some concentrations it is not at others. Plants must obtain chemicals from the soil, for example nitrogen, phosphorus, potash, iron and boron, and without these chemicals they would die or be very unhealthy. There are two points being made here: firstly that chemicals *per se* are not necessarily harmful and secondly, that in the case of harmful chemicals (such as CO_2) it is the concentration at which it is used which determines the harm it may do.

Man has always added chemicals to his fields. In early days he used excreta, dung and bones. He sprayed and fumigated his plants with urine, sulphur, pitch and many other substances, was little the worse for it and probably was much better fed. The chemical problem really arose when man discovered how to make chemicals—this was looked on as being unnatural. It is a surprising thought that most of us are willing to take synthetic antibiotics and medicines, to dress in synthetic fibres, and to use chemical disinfectants, household powders and so on, but at the same time will raise our hands in horror if chemicals are used on crops or to feed animals. Man of course has never been particularly logical, and there are still many who will swear that there is a chemical difference between the Vitamin C in black-currant juice and that in the tablets you can buy in any chemist, although they are unable to tell you wherein this chemical difference lies.

Gardeners can rest assured that the plant cannot distinguish between nitrates if they are derived from artificially-made chemicals or from bacterial degradation of farm-yard manure. Where then do the dangers to the environment lie in the use of artificial fertilisers? They lie in the belief that if you want to obtain the best crops *and* keep your soil in good condition all you need to use is artificials. This is *not* so for soil needs humus if a good soil structure is to be maintained. Danger can also lie in the application of nitrogenous or phosphatic fertilisers in excess, for what the plants can't use is washed out in the drainage water, gets into lakes and rivers and may cause such excessive plant growth there that the fish are deprived of oxygen and die. Once again the moral is clear, using fertilisers in excess is not only uneconomic but could be harmful.

However, the real worry of environmentalists in relation to the garden lies in the use of pesticides, fungicides and weed-killers and the effect they might have on the balance of nature. Once again historically many substances have been used such as sulphur, tar and nicotine dust and although they are partly produced by other living things (derris, pyrethrin) the insects they kill are just as dead as if they had been killed by DDT. *Any* insecticide, fungicide or weed-killer will upset the balance of nature, for that is their fundamental purpose. The two properties of modern chemicals which create the fear of environmental destruction is their persistence and their remarkable efficiency.

Concern about the persistence of insecticides began when traces of DDT, which does not occur naturally, were found in all sorts of unexpected places, from penguins in the Antarctic to human beings in the north of Canada. DDT can only have got into the many diverse places in which it is now found by being incorporated into food chains which can stretch from an English garden via drainage water to the sea, from there into tiny sea plants and animals, hence into fish and so into penguins (and man) who eat the fish. DDT kills insects and if the insects are eaten by birds then it enters another food chain and there are links claimed between the decline in fertility of birds of prey and the treatment of seed corn with insecticides such as Aldrin.

Because it is so persistent there are very justifiable fears that a chemical such as DDT might slowly accumulate at the ends of food chains and, since so many of these end in man, there is great concern about their ultimate effect on the human race. Of course nobody can predict the *ultimate* effect of anything which slowly accumulates. It took nearly one hundred years to discover that smoking was a strong contributory factor in lung cancer, and there is some evidence that animal fats including butter contribute to heart disease, and what the ultimate effect of that may be, in terms of the human race, is impossible to judge. I would suggest that, since we can't know the ultimate effect of anything, this is no reason for doing nothing at all, but is a very good reason for proceeding with care and only after making such checks as are possible within reason.

There is a further problem which arises from the efficiency of many insecticides, namely, that, since they kill so very well, they will affect the balance of nature particularly strongly, and this may lead anywhere. The essential difficulty in this argument is that the 'anywhere' envisaged is always a very bad or, at best, a worse situation. In this discussion it must always be remembered that evolution is a process of change, and that nature has never stood still. Species come and go. The great dinosaurs arrived and dominated the earth and they then vanished almost completely and have been replaced by other animals. Giant horsetails formed the dominant vegetation in the Carboniferous period, but now all that is left of this species are a few pernicious garden weeds. Change is essential and it would be wrong to try to prevent it by fossilising the *status quo*. This is not to say that the unrestricted or uncontrolled use of chemicals is a good thing, for there is enough evidence to show that it is not; it is important to avoid major, even if local, upsets in the continued existence of life. How can the amateur gardener do this? He must at all times practise garden hygiene by destroying diseased plants or plant parts, he must make sure that any plants he buys are clean and healthy, and he must endeavour to keep as much humus in his soil as possible in order to encourage earthworms, soil insects and bacteria, and to keep the soil in good physical condition. Above all he should use chemicals at the correct times and in the recommended quantities, for using them to excess or at the wrong time of year can not only harm the environment but it can prove a waste of hard-earned money. Thus the best place for fertilisers and especially phosphates is in the seed bed. To apply sulphate of ammonia when the crop is not growing is simply pouring money down a drain and the nitrogen may begin to damage stream and pond life if it is applied in excess.

Common problems and queries

1. *Is it possible to control all the factors in the environment and so obtain a perfect crop?*
It is certainly possible to control factors such as heat, light, humidity, CO content, feeding, and pest and disease control, and by careful spacing of the crop to get very high yields indeed. But although the means are available with automatic switches controlling different factors working on the same principle as the thermostat, to control everything would require very intricate and sophisticated technology and the starting point would have to be a completely dark closed building, well insulated, and with an artificial atmosphere geared to the maximum photo-

T.Y.B.O.G.—8

synthesis. The real difficulty in such a set-up is not the technology but the cost, especially of the electricity consumed to keep the environment exactly right as the plants grow and develop. It becomes more and more likely that the cost of the energy which such a system would require would be greater than the value of the increased yields over traditional methods. For example, the sun heats and lights a traditional greenhouse for nothing, but if the sun were to be replaced by electricity then the cost of production might soar.

There is also a technical difficulty which is not related to the physical conditions but to the plants themselves, for as a plant grows, the demands it makes on the environment change and our knowledge of this subject is rather fragmentary and generalised at the moment. It is also probable that each variety of every crop would have different requirements and an enormous body of data would have to be amassed before the perfect crop could be grown. It would certainly be more rewarding to make better use of existing knowledge for the standard of production in many fields or gardens is very much lower than it ought to be. This question raises another point of considerable importance, namely, should ordinary gardeners try to obtain the *maximum* from the soil or should they try to obtain the *best*? These may be very different for it is often easy to grow big crops of inferior varieties while the high quality varieties may be low yielding but of excellent flavour or scent or colour. In general the gardener must grow what he and his family like, but if a choice had to be made I would let the commercial people grow the mass-market crops because they yield well, keep well, have good colour, and so on. In the garden I would grow plants which I could not get in the shops even if I could afford them. Thus I would grow Cox's Orange Pippin rather than Golden Delicious apples.

2. *Is it true that if frosted plants are sprayed with cold water before they thaw they will not suffer from frost damage?*
This is the kind of question to which the answer must be both 'yes' and 'no' for it depends on the severity of the frost and when the spraying is done. Certainly plants which have been

deeply frozen will suffer damage no matter what you do, so the answer for them is that spraying with water will not help. Plants touched by overnight frost, say, at the end of April or the beginning of May, can be saved by this spray technique. The reason is that plants suffer much more severely from being quickly thawed than from being frosted. It was said that frost damage largely arose from ice formation in the plant, but if the thawing process is slow it seems that any damage done can be healed during the thawing process, but a quick thaw gives no time for healing and a permanent injury follows.

The question now becomes one of how sprayed water can slow down the rate of thawing. It must be remembered that as water freezes it gives off heat. Plants lightly frozen and having a thin film of water sprayed on them will actually get heat from the film as it freezes on the surface and so they will begin to thaw slowly. Then as the day warms up the thaw will be completed and with any luck the plant will be undamaged.

3. How do rain and floods affect the use of fertilisers?
The fact is that it is usually rain which washes fertilisers out of the soil but because we tend to accept this, attention is only drawn to the losses after floods. The gradual loss of materials from the soil is termed *leaching* and it forms a very important side of fertiliser use. Plants absorb minerals from the soil in the form of salts dissolved in water. But salts dissolved in water move down through the soil, get into the drains and eventually into rivers, lakes and seas.

It is a kind of race between the speed at which the plants can absorb the salts and the speed at which rain and floods will wash them out. The plants can be helped by using lots of compost for this absorbs the salts and prevents them being leached away. The use of slow-release fertilisers is also helpful for they only release their mineral salts over a period of months so they cannot be washed away by a single rainstorm or flood. However, these fertilisers are not unmixed blessings for if the release is very slow the crop may be out of the ground before all the fertiliser has been used up. To get full value therefore they should be used on permanent or semi-permanent subjects such as rose bushes, shrubs, and perennials. In the vegetable garden they are useful if the soil is going to be occupied by successional crops such as Brussels sprouts after the early potatoes have been lifted.

The chemical most quickly washed from the soil is nitrogen. This means that a shortage of nitrogen can arise very quickly and most crops will respond almost immediately to an application of a nitrogen-containing fertiliser such as sulphate of ammonia, nitrate of soda or dried blood. Other elements such as phosphates, potash, boron or iron are only lost very slowly if at all so that they do not require replacement at anything like the same rate as nitrogen.

4. *Will a well-grown plant be able to resist or be immune to pests and diseases?*
There is no doubt that resistance to many plant pests and diseases is considerably increased if the plants are well grown. It is also true to say that a well-fed plant may yield a good crop *despite* attacks by fungi or insects. True natural immunity however is an inbred (or genetic) quality and although the expression of characteristics is influenced by the environment and may be raised to its highest level under ideal conditions, the maximum immunity which a plant can show is fixed by its genetic potential. Another factor which should always be remembered is that plants like humans have no qualities which make them immune to every threat. For example our vaccinations which confer immunity against, say, smallpox, will have no effect on polio and we require another series of injections to give us immunity to the latter disease. By the same token if plant breeders produce a rose immune from mildew they have to go on to try to add resistance to black spot to that already present. In other words practically all pests and diseases have to be tackled separately.

It is generally accepted that feeding with nitrogenous fertilisers to excess will reduce disease and pest resistance. There are many reasons for this including (1) nitrogen increases the size of plants so they will become more crowded in the drill and so create a microclimate more favourable for the spread of disease, (2) such plants stay soft and green longer and so increase the time available for infection or attack, (3) nitrogen delays the time of flowering and setting fruit so that the crop may persist into a time of year which favours the disease by virtue of temperature or humidity changes. It is commonly accepted that fertilisers containing phosphate and potash seem to increase resistance but it is much more likely that what they do is counterbalance excess nitrogen. It still remains absolutely invaluable advice to gardeners to try to grow crops to the highest standard, for by so doing they will be giving themselves the chance of harvesting a good crop despite the many pests and diseases.

Glossary

Cross references are shown in small capitals

Activator: A substance (usually containing nitrogen) added to a compost heap to speed up the bacterial formation of HUMUS.

Air drainage: The ability of air to move freely through or across a crop. Such drainage is much affected by crop and plant spacing, or by hedges, buildings, or land contours.

Algae: Green plants whose natural environment is usually very moist. They are non-flowering and often microscopic.

Angiosperms: Flowering plants.

Annual: A plant whose entire life cycle from seed to seed is complete in one year. Once the plant produces seed it dies.

Anthers: The yellow club-like structures in a flower. They contain the male cells, the POLLEN.

Anti-transpirant: A substance which when sprayed on leaves will very much reduce the rate of water loss. Anti-transpirants are widely used when transplanting.

Aphid: GREENFLY.

Axil: The angle made by the leaf stalk with the stem.

Axillary Bud: The bud which is invariably present in the leaf axil.

Bacteria: Small one-celled organisms which are almost universal and are responsible for many decay processes and disease conditions.

Biological control: The limitation by one living thing of the growth or reproduction of another. Ladybirds which eat greenfly are acting as a form of biological control.

Biotic: Used to describe a factor, for example in the environment, which has its origin in a living organism. Thus a pest or disease is a biotic factor in the environment of a host.

Botrytis: A fungus which causes a very common grey mould disease and is encouraged by damp conditions.

Brassicas: The Brassica family which includes cabbage, cauliflower, sprouts and kale.

138

Budding: The process whereby a bud of one variety of a plant is made to grow on the stem of a second variety. Once the bud is established the rest of the stem of the second variety is cut away and so the aerial part of the plant is of a different variety from the root system. Common in rose growing.

Calcifuge: Plants such as rhododendrons which cannot be grown well if there is calcium (lime, chalk) in the soil.

Callus: Cells which form when a wound is made in a plant. These cells have great potentialities and may heal the wound or produce roots or buds.

Calyx: The green (usually) structures which form the outermost ring of floral parts. Individual calyx parts are called sepals.

Cambium: The layer of rapidly dividing cells which lies between xylem and phloem in a stem and which is responsible for the fusion of GRAFTS, BUDDINGS, and for the production of many plant tissues.

Capping: (*a*) The hard crust which may form on the surface of the soil if it dries out too quickly.

(*b*) Putting a layer of soil (or even a sheet of plastic) over a compost heap.

Chelated compound: A chemical in which the metallic element, for example iron, is so combined that plants can obtain sufficient of the necessary element without it being 'fixed' in a chalk or limestone soil.

Chlorophyll: The green colouring material in plants which is responsible for the use of light energy in PHOTOSYNTHESIS.

Chloroplast: Disc-shaped bodies in plant tissue which contain chlorophyll.

Chlorotic: Pale green or yellow leaves due often to iron deficiency.

Club root: A disease of Brassicas caused by a fungus which produces swellings (clubs) on the roots and so can deprive the plant of both food and water.

Compost: (*a*) The humus rich material produced by bacterial action on decaying vegetation, often in a compost heap.

(*b*) Medium put in pots or seed boxes usually containing soil, peat and sand.

Conditioner: A chemical substance which will improve soil structure by increasing the rate of crumb formation.

Crumb: Used to denote the aggregation of smaller soil particles into a larger unit. Produced by liming clay soils and by the action of HUMUS, BACTERIA and FUNGI.

Cutting: Part of a stem which when detached from the parent plant and put under good soil conditions will produce roots and can be grown as a separate plant.

Damping-off: A disease which attacks and kills seedlings when they are over-watered or growing too thickly together. Best controlled by using sterile seed compost and avoiding over-planting.

Day neutral: Applied to plants whose time of flowering is *not* controlled by day length. Many weeds, for example the daisy, are day neutral.

Dazomet: A soil disinfectant.

Drawn: Plants which are tall and spindly usually as a result of being grown in inadequate light.

Drift: The uncontrolled spread of chemicals, for example weedkillers, usually caused by wind.

Drill: A shallow furrow or trench into which seeds are sown.

Drip line: The imaginary line on the ground beneath a tree where leaves would shed drips and along which the tree should be fed.

Embryo: The very young organism which is formed immediately after the fusion of sex cells, for example pollen and ovule.

Encarsia formosa: A tiny wasp which eats whitefly and which can be used as a form of biological control in enclosed areas.

Enzymes: Chemical substances produced by living organisms by means of which they perform most chemical reactions.

Etiolated: Term applied to plants grown in the dark which have yellowish leaves and long, weak, straggly stems.

F1 Hybrid: A strongly-growing high-yielding plant produced by interbreeding two pure strains.

Fibrous roots: The system of fine feeding roots often produced relatively near the soil surface.

Foliar feed: A mixture of food-supplying chemicals which, when sprayed on the leaves, will be directly absorbed. Of use in situations where the soil may be reactive with ordinary chemicals applied via the soil to the roots.

Friendly insects: Insects such as ladybirds which parasitise or eat plant pests. They are important as a means of biological control.

Fumigate: To use an insecticidal or fungicidal smoke to kill pests or diseases in an enclosed area, for example a greenhouse.

Fungi: Fine thread-like plants which, because they have no chlorophyll, are obliged to obtain their food from other living or dead organisms. Typical fungi are moulds, mildews, rusts, blights and even mushrooms.

Fungicide: Any chemical which will kill fungi. The original ones contained copper, mercury and arsenic, but much safer sprays are now available.

Germination: The initial stages in the development of a plant from a seed.

Girdle: To remove, or partly remove, a ring of bark from the trunk of a tree. In expert hands partial girdling can be used to induce fruit bearing. Can kill the tree.

Graft: The union of a rootstock with another plant (SCION) in order to control the growth of the final product. Many fruit trees are grafted as also are lilacs and rhododendrons.

Greenfly: APHIDS. Small insects which suck their food from the leaves of plants. They also spread virus diseases.

Greenhouse effect: The phenomenon whereby light energy is stored as heat and so raises greenhouse temperatures.

Grey mould: The common name for the disease produced by Botrytis. Controlled by sulphur, captan, benlate.

Growth chamber: A totally enclosed room for growing plants. Usually all the factors of the environment, for example light, humidity and temperature, are automatically controlled.

Guard cell: One of the two cells whose movements control the size of the aperture of a STOMA.

Hardening off: The process whereby plants raised in a protected environment are gradually acclimatised to colder outdoor conditions.

Hormone: Literally a 'chemical messenger' whereby one part of an organism controls the growth of a distant part. Hormones in plants are often produced in growing tips but affect structures lower down the stem.

Humidity: The amount of moisture held by the air.

Humus: The dark coloured substance produced by bacterial breakdown of organic material which is of great importance in soil.

Hydroponics: Growing plants without soil and usually in a solution of nutritive salts.

Inbred: Since many flowers are bisexual it is possible for a plant to pollinate and fertilise itself. The seed so produced and the plants from that seed are said to constitute an *inbred line*.

Insecticide: A chemical which kills insects.

Internode: The length of stem between successive leaf AXILS (NODES).

Iron deficiency: A diseased condition arising from a lack of available iron in the soil (usually chalk or limestone soil). The symptoms are yellowing leaves and reduced yield. FOLIAR FEEDING is advised or the use of CHELATES.

Lean-to: A greenhouse one of whose walls forms part of an existing structure, for example, the main house.

Leguminoseae: The group of plants which contain peas, beans and clovers.

Microclimate: The environmental conditions in a very limited area, for example, within a potato crop, in a seed box, in a very sheltered corner of a garden.

Monitoring: Continuously checking the levels of some specific factor, for example, thermostats monitor temperature.

Mosaic: The occurrence of yellow patches on leaves caused by a virus disease.

Mulch: Material used to protect and cover the soil surface. Most mulches are ORGANIC but black polythene sheeting is being increasingly used.

Nicking: Cutting a piece out of the seed coat of hard seed such as sweet-pea.

Node: The point at which the leaf stalk meets the stem. This is the site of the LEAF AXIL and the AXILLARY BUD.

No-soil compost: Because soil is very variable and is often in short supply, composts have been developed which are mixtures of sand and peat with fertiliser added.

Organic matter: Any material derived from anything which has formed the whole or part of a living organism.

Overlap: The area where two sheets (usually of glass) lie on top of each other. This is a nice example of a MICROCLIMATE.

Over-stocking: Crowding too many plants into a limited area.

Ovule: The structure which contains the actual egg cell.

Paraquat: A very poisonous but short-lived and highly effective weed-killer.

Perennial: A plant which lives for many years. Strictly speaking trees, shrubs and other plants such as Michaelmas daisies are perennials.

Pest: Usually applied to insects which damage plants.

Petals: The brightly coloured parts of a flower. Technically the ring of structures between the CALYX and the ANTHERS.

pH: A scale used to express the acidity or alkalinity of a soil. In this scale pH 6.8 is neutral, lower numbers are acidic and higher numbers are alkaline.

Phloem: A system of cells which ramify through the plant and are the primary channel for the transport of food.

Photoperiodicity: The phenomenon of the control of flowering by the length of the light and dark periods.

Photosynthesis: A chemical process whereby CO_2 and H_2O are used by chlorophyll in the presence of light to form much more complex organic substances such as starches or sugars.

Phytochrome: A pigment in plants which is sensitive to light and which forms the basis of the phenomenon of PHOTOPERIODICITY.

Pollen: The yellow dust contained in the anthers. Each pollen grain can act as the male fertile cell.

Pollination: The transference of pollen to the stigma which is a necessary preliminary to fertilisation.

Pricking-out: When seedlings have grown a little they require room for further growth. This room is given by re-planting the seedlings in rows in a box filled with compost. This is known as pricking-out.

Reproductive parts: Generally the parts and products of the flower.

Rhizome: A stem which grows along under the ground.

Ringing, Ring barking: See GIRDLE.

Root hair: Long but fine cells produced near the tip of roots. These root hairs are the means by which the plant absorbs water and mineral salts.

Root nodule: Swellings filled with bacteria on the roots of leguminous plants. These bacteria can extract (fix) nitrogen from the air and make it available for plant use.

Root run: The area of soil in which the roots grow.

Rootstock: In a grafted plant the rootstock provides the root system for the SCION.

Rotation: A system of cultivation which ensures that the same crop does *not* occupy the same area of ground in successive years. The most common rotations are of three or four years.

Scion: The above-ground part of a grafted plant.

Scorch: The appearance of dry, usually brown, areas on a leaf. Can be caused by heat, drought, chemicals, trace element deficiency.

Selective weed-killer: A chemical which when applied to mixed herbage (for example a weedy lawn) will kill some kinds of plants (the weeds) and leave others (the grass) unharmed.

Self-fertilisation: See INBRED.

Sensor: A device for detecting changes in certain environmental factors, for example humidity sensors would be used to regulate atmospheric humidity in a GROWTH CHAMBER.

Sepal: See CALYX.

Sequestrene: A type of chemical compound which is not 'fixed' by the soil. See CHELATED COMPOUNDS.

Short-day plant: A plant which will only flower when the days are less than twelve hours long, for example chrysanthemum.

Slow-release fertiliser: A fertiliser made up in the form of granules which only dissolve slowly in the soil solution. It is therefore available to plants over a long period.

Soil cable: High resistance electric cable covered with insulating materials. The heat produced by the current can be used to raise soil temperatures.

Specimen tree: A tree given enough room to develop its natural shape and size without competition from other trees.

Spindly: Thin and weak.

Sterile: Unable to produce fertile seed. This may be due to lack of flowers or other reasons but because of VEGETATIVE PROPAGATION sterile plants can be multiplied.

Stigma: The sticky top of the STYLE where the pollen lands.

Stolon: A stem which grows parallel to and on the surface of the ground.

Stoma(ta): One of the pores usually found on leaves through which gases and water vapour enter and leave the leaf (see GUARD CELLS).

Style: The usually tubular extension of the ovaries which terminates in the STIGMA.

Systemic: Permeating the whole system of the plant.

Tap root: The main root which penetrates deeply into the soil.

Trace element: An element only needed in very small quantity, but the absence of which can lead to deficiency diseases and early death of the plant. Trace elements include iron, boron, manganese, zinc, molybdenum.

Transpiration: The loss of water from a leaf generally through the STOMATA.

Tuber: A swollen underground stem used for food storage.

Vegetative parts: All parts of the plant with the exception of the flower.

Vegetative propagation: All means of plant propagation in which vegetative parts are used. These include cuttings, bulbs, tubers, offsets, stolons.

Virus: A sub-microscopic entity whose presence is only detected when it produces disease symptoms. There are many virus diseases and since there is no control, affected plants should be uprooted and burned. They are generally spread by insects especially aphids.

Weed host: Plants where pests and diseases may shelter when there is no crop in the ground.

Whitefly: A very common greenhouse pest which can be chemically controlled with resmethrin.

Wilt: A disease usually of the root system whose main symptom is wilting.

Wilting: The collapse of the rigidity of leaves usually due to a lack of water or a wilt disease.

Xylem: The central woody tissue of the stem which is the main water-conducting channel.

Further Reading

A. J. Biggs, *Growing Vegetables*, Hodder & Stoughton (Teach Yourself), 1979.
Alan Brook, *The Living Plant*, Edinburgh University Press, 1964.
A. E. Canham, *Electricity in Horticulture*, Churchill, 1964.
J. Escritt, *Lawns*, Hodder & Stoughton (Teach Yourself), 1979.
A. R. Gemmell, *The Practical Gardener's Encyclopedia*, Collins, 1977.
R. Genders, *Growing Fruit*, Hodder & Stoughton (Teach Yourself), 1979.
C. Hart, *Greenhouses*, Hodder & Stoughton (Teach Yourself), 1980.
P. Hemsley, *Growing Trees and Shrubs* (Teach Yourself), 1979.
A. D. Imms, *Insect Natural History*, Fontana (New Naturalist), 1973.
W. O. James, *Background to Gardening*, Allen & Unwin, 1957.
H. Maddox, *Your Garden Soil*, David & Charles, 1974.
K. Paisley, *Fertilisers and Manures*, Collingridge 1960.
Sir E. J. Russell, *The World of the Soil*, Fontana (New Naturalist), 1961.
K. Whitehead, *Garden Flowers*, Hodder & Stoughton (Teach Yourself), 1979.

Metric/Imperial Equivalents

Temperature

°F	°C
45	7
50	10
55	13
60	16
65	18
70	21

Length

in	cm
$\frac{1}{4}$	0·5
$\frac{1}{2}$	1·0
1	2·5
12	30
24	60

Weight

oz/sq yd	g/m²	oz	g
1	35	1	28
2	70	4	113
3	100	16 (1 lb)	454
4	140	36 ($2\frac{1}{4}$ lb)	1000 (1 Kg)

Area

1 sq yd = 0·8 m²
$1\frac{1}{4}$ sq yd = 1·0 m²

Volume

pints	litres
$\frac{1}{2}$	0·3
1	0·6
$1\frac{3}{4}$	1·0

Note: These conversions are approximate.

Index

GROWING VEGETABLES

TONY BIGGS

Everything you could want to know about vegetables from planning your vegetable garden, soils and plant nutrition, principles of crop rotation to crop harvesting and storage, and a summary of what to do when round the year.

This is a book for all gardeners whether you have a walled kitchen garden or only a windowsill, patio or roof-garden. The beginner will find the basic approach particularly helpful but there is also a wealth of useful information for the experienced gardener.

Tony Biggs is Lecturer in Horticulture, Wye College, University of London where his speciality is vegetable crops. Besides lecturing and researching on the subject he is also a keen gardener and his family are self-sufficient in vegetables.

TEACH YOURSELF BOOKS